ONE MAKES THE DIFFERENCE

ONE MAKES THE DIFFERENCE

inspiring actions that change our world

Julia Butterfly Hill

and Jessica Hurley

HarperSanFrancisco

A Division of HarperCollins*Publishers*

The authors would like to extend special thanks to Oxygen Media, the Goldman Prize Foundation, the Giraffe Project, and the Odyssey World Trek for providing select inspirational stories and materials for this book.

A percentage of the author's proceeds are being donated to the causes that are highlighted in this book.

ONE MAKES THE DIFFERENCE: *Inspiring Actions That Change Our World.* Copyright © 2002 by Julia Butterfly Hill. All rights reserved. Printed in the United States of America. No part of this book may be used or reproduced in any manner whatsoever without written permission except in the case of brief quotations embodied in critical articles and reviews. For information address HarperCollins Publishers, Inc., 10 East 53rd Street, New York, NY 10022.

HarperCollins books may be purchased for educational, business, or sales promotional use. For information please write: Special Markets Department, HarperCollins Publishers, Inc., 10 East 53rd Street, New York, NY 10022.

HarperCollins Web site: http://www.harpercollins.com

HarperCollins®, ■®, and HarperSanFrancisco™ are trademarks of HarperCollins Publishers, Inc.

FIRST EDITION

Library of Congress Cataloging-in-Publication Data

Hill, Julia Butterfly.
 One makes the difference : inspiring actions that change our world / by Julia Butterfly Hill and Jessica Hurley.
 p. cm.
 ISBN 0-06-251756-2 (pbk. : alk. paper)
 1. Environmental responsibility. 2. Environmental protection. I. Hurley, Jessica. II. Title.
GE195.7.H55 2001
333.7'2—dc21 2001051542

02 03 04 05 06 ❖/RRD(H) 10 9 8 7 6 5 4 3 2 1

This book is dedicated to you, the reader,
deciding to live Love in Action and helping others to do the same.

And to the incredible spirit of all the unsung heroes of the world
who see an injustice and decide to be the one to make the difference.
They, and this beautiful Earth, are our inspiration.

CONTENTS

ACKNOWLEDGMENTS

From Julia

When I begin to make lists of the people I am grateful to, I have enough names to fill an entire book. As a few acknowledgment pages could not possibly hold all of my appreciation listed individually, I instead would like to just say simply, "Thank You" to all of you who are in this book, all of you who helped with this book, everyone who is doing good in the world, everyone who has supported and loved me throughout my life, and even those who have not. You have all been great teachers to me. May you feel all the love and gratitude I have for you. A very special thanks to Jessica Hurley and Kavitha Rao, without whom this book would not be.

I send deep prayers to the indigenous peoples of this country and the world who hold the sacred understanding of the interconnection of life and are suffering and dying as the Earth, in all of its forms, suffers and is destroyed. I offer my life in humble dedication to justice for every person, animal, forest, and place—every aspect of life—because I know between us, there is no separation.

It is to this I say with the deepest love, gratitude, respect, and actions, "To all my relations."

From Jessica

Jessica would like to thank all of the amazing people gracing the pages of this book, as well as the unsung heroes, for truly making the difference in our world!

Julia, for your infinite inspiration and dedication. Kavitha Rao, our research associate and environmental consultant extraordinaire. My dear sister Miriam, for exquisite fact checking and editing in the eleventh hour. Sweet Christopher, for sharing your extensive knowledge base and wordsmithing skills, but mainly for nourishing my body and spirit when I needed it most.

Liz Perle, our fabulous (and patient) editor, for providing the "pruning" and light that helped our word garden grow, and to Rebecca, Nicole, Terri, Priscilla, Anne, Kyran, Chris, and the rest of the Harper San Francisco crew, for seeing it through. PB and Kris, for all of your hard work. The Goldman Environmental Prize Foundation and Giraffe.org, for honoring those who truly deserve it. Greggie and Chumbe Coral Park, for insight into the underwater world. Abeja (and the Odyssey World Trek), for your editing contributions and story sharing. Dana Smirin, for your intuition and perseverance. Dawn and Dana, for great suggestions. Dixie and Kristin, for "being fearless." Axel, for your very generous contribution to this project. Lynnie, for being my mental mentor. Mossy-poo, a top-notch concierge.

Jakoji Zen Center, for giving me an inspirational retreat and peace of mind. Joseph at SafariMakers, for sharing the wildlife of the Serengeti. Bobby from the EPA, for letting me pick your brain on the plane. Oh, and the librarian who let me keep the books out way longer than I should have.

Grandpa Arthur and Mrs. Hanley (my tenth-grade biology teacher), who always wanted me to work in the sciences. My parents, who raised me quite literally under the earth and taught me at an early age the value of living harmoniously with the environment. Rosetta, Miriam ("The Elder"), and Aunt Celia, for helping me to reconsider. Gabe, Erin, Katy-cat, Schmudie, XT, Schmarina, Gali, KC, Kitten, Lenira, my Campalicious and Houseboat tribes, Reilly (and Joe), Judy, Dr. Nadler, my team at ThriveOnline on Oxygen, my UPN crew, and the rest of my family and friends who provided me with endless support.

A special dedication to Pat and the rest of my ex-co-workers at Tyco Toys/View-Master/Mattel, who, to date, have been unable to prove that their kidney cancers and other health problems are related to the high levels of the "possible human carcinogen" TCE found in our well's drinking water supply.

INTRODUCTION

Spirit Makes the Difference

If you think you're too small to be effective, you have never been in bed with a mosquito.

—BETTE REESE

Let the beauty we love be what we do.
There are hundreds of ways to kneel and kiss the ground.

—RUMI

This is a book about love. A book about love in action. It is that simple. And it is that profound.

The first twenty-three years of my life on this Earth were filled with the struggles common to young people interwoven with my own unique experiences, difficulties, triumphs, heartbreak, and joy. From the moment of my birth, my family taught me that being good, believing in God, and being "saved" were the most important things I would ever do with my life. Society taught me that getting good grades so I could go to a good college so I could get a good job and make good money and spend even more were the most important things I would ever do with my life. "Good" in whose eyes? Until I reached my teens, I followed what was virtuous in my parents' eyes. They would tell you that I did what was good in God's eyes.

When I became a teenager, I did what every good child of that age does—I rebelled. I was very attracted by other rebels; though, they were mostly the ones without a clue or a cause. Then I bought right into the sales pitch of the American economic system and began to work very hard to be good in society's eyes. My life's value was based on how much money I could make and spend, what I looked like, and how others perceived me. I lived this way until a severe car wreck altered my life. This intense experience changed the way I viewed the world and my place in it. My spirituality broke free from the confines of my parents' religion, and my heart overflowed with a desire to find my true purpose in this life. Not the supposed purpose placed upon me by others, but the purpose intrinsic to who I am—the purpose given to me by the Creator.

Why I am here? Why am I alive? These questions led me on a quest. This search then led me to northern California, where I experienced a deeply spiritual epiphany when I entered the majestic cathedral of a redwood forest. I saw God as I had never believed possible—in the trees, in the ferns, moss, and mushrooms, in the air and water, birds and bears. I finally saw God with all of my senses, with all of who I am, from the inside out. God, both male and female. God, more than male, more than female. God of all life, in all of its forms.

When I found out that 97 percent of the original redwoods had already been cut down, and that the little left was still being destroyed in an extremely toxic and devastating way, I was sickened, heartbroken, and angrier than I can ever remember being. How could this be happening in "America the Beautiful"? My naïveté was washed away by my flood of tears. I had seen what was beautiful, profound, sacred. Then I saw that the Sacred was being destroyed. I knew I had to do something to try to stop it.

When I first began to consider getting involved with the environmental issue, I—being the human that I am—came up with 101 reasons why I could not, and should not, take action. Reasons like, "I don't know enough or have enough experience." Or, "There are plenty of people working on this issue, so I should just go on my planned travels to find my sought-after purpose in life." I have since learned that anytime we come up with excuses why we can't or shouldn't do something, it's usually because we are afraid that we can and that we will do it. In my prayers, I received a message loud and clear: "Julia, if you walk away from this injustice, your inactions will be as much a part of the destruction of the redwoods as the actions of the CEOs of those lumber companies." Over and over in my mind like a mantra: *My inactions are a part of the injustice in the world, just as surely as the actions and inactions of others.*

I ended up climbing into a redwood tree, estimated to be more than one thousand years old, that was marked to be cut down by the Maxxam-controlled Pacific Lumber Company. I had planned on staying in the tree for three weeks to a month. I wound up living in it for 738 days without ever once touching the ground. I did this in order to protect this tree called Luna and to bring attention to the destruction of our old-growth forests around the world. During my time perched in this magnificent tree, I gained a whole new view of our world. I saw intimately how interconnected *all* of life truly is and how everything we do affects this beautiful planet and us, the people and animals who call it home. This book is about learning what is wrong and what is right and finding the love and power to decide to do something about it.

We have become so good at pinpointing what is wrong in the world, and yet these problems are reflections of our actions and behaviors. With so much of our cultural and natural world being destroyed, mutilated, and oppressed, everywhere we look we can catalog the issues that urgently need to be addressed before it's too late. But every time we point out the damage being done, there are still three fingers pointing right back at us. When we point at what is wrong, we must take responsibility and try to embody and enact what is right. For me, these digits pointing in our own direction stand for *power, responsibility, and love* in our daily life, community life, and global life.

The first finger represents *power.* We are *all* powerful beyond our wildest imaginations. We have been conditioned, numbed, and manipulated over time into giving our power away to name brands, corporations, and governmental officials, just for starters. It's time we take the power back!

We have the power to change the world. *Everything* we do and say does change the world. Even our inactions have impact. If I had walked away from the destruction of the redwoods without trying to stop it, my inactions would have had as much adverse impact as my decision to live in a threatened ancient redwood tree. In every moment of every day we make choices, and every choice has an impact, positive or negative. We are moving either toward the problem or toward the solution.

The second finger stands for *responsibility.* Because we are beings of tremendous power and energy, we have the responsibility to choose carefully, compassionately, courageously, and consciously. We have become addicted to, and transfixed by, our right and freedom to choose. Yet, all the while, we accept less and less of the responsibility for the impact of our decisions and how those decisions ripple out and affect the planet, its people, and the future. Every time we do not take responsibility for our choices, some other person or place is paying the price for it—and that price is high. Compound interest is not just an economic reality; it is inherent in the equation of life.

The third finger symbolizes *love*. Why love? Why not! What else would we want to do with our lives than offer them in loving joyous service to the Earth and *all* its inhabitants? With love, hatred and anger transform into fierce compassion; struggles and challenges become opportunities for growth and strength. Responsibility transforms from drudgery and necessary evil into a newfound happiness in our ability to respond. The greatest, most positive, and longest-lasting change will always come from a shift in consciousness in the heart.

As we point out all that is wrong in the world and see the three fingers—power, responsibility, and love—pointing back, we realize they lie in the palms of our own hands. Our ability to change the world lies in our hands, minds, hearts, bodies, and spirits—committed in action. It's not only that we *can* make a difference, it's that we *do* make the difference. The kind of change we make is up to us. Each and every one of us has the power to heal or to hurt, to be the hero or the destroyer—with every moment, with every breath of every day.

My prayer for you, for the Earth, and for this book is that when the final page has been turned, you will have found the information, inspiration, and helpful connections you need to be one who makes the difference. That your heart will be open to your courage, compassion, respect and, most important, to the *love* that lies within your highest self. And that you will step boldly and joyously into the healer and the hero that you already are within.

Julia Butterfly Hill
June 2001

ONE

Making the Difference

Until one is committed there is always hesitancy, the chance to draw back, always ineffectiveness. Concerning all acts of initiative (and creation), there is one elementary truth—ignorance of which kills countless ideas and splendid plans: That the moment one definitely commits oneself, then Providence moves too. All sorts of things occur to help one that would never otherwise have occurred. A whole stream of events and issues from the decision, raising in one's favor all manners of unforeseen incidents and meetings and material assistance, which no man could have dreamed would come his way.

Whatever you can do,
or dream you can, begin it.
Boldness has genius,
power, and magic in it.
Begin it now.

—JOHANN WOLFGANG VON GOETHE

Our country was founded on some unassailable values. In our Declaration of Independence it says that we have inalienable rights to life, liberty, and the pursuit of happiness. This book, which you may think is about the Earth, is about more than that. It is about these fundamental principles—about living freely and joyfully on a planet that is treated as responsibly as we ourselves wish to be treated. This is a book about the freedom to choose and the freedom to act. This is a book whose aim it is to open our eyes and hearts so that we define happiness as more than what we own or what we wear or how easy it is to buy, and get, and spend.

Throughout our history, we have struggled to maintain these privileges of freedom, choice, and self-determination. We have never backed down from protecting these rights, but have taken the actions we needed to protect what we so value. Now it is time to take these values and principles and apply them to our planet.

Many of us have already begun to take steps to reverse the damage done by pollution and waste, but many more of us, when confronted with the size of some of these problems, sigh and feel we just can't make a difference.

Well, the truth is you can do it. And you must. The greatest act of self-love and love for the Earth is to take one step at a time. The following pages will explain some of the greatest threats to our environment, will provide inspirational stories about people who found the courage to act on their concerns, and will give you loving actions you can take to help save the planet. The actions here can be practiced by all, young and old. All that matters is that we take them.

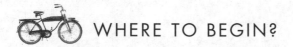

WHERE TO BEGIN?

Better to light a candle than to curse the darkness.

—CHINESE PROVERB

Many people are paralyzed by the number of environmental burdens placed upon our planet. They want to make a difference, but it seems so overwhelming that they quit before taking the first step. In actuality, there are only two places to start: in your head and in your heart. When you choose to become educated on environmental problems and solutions, you start with your head. And, once ignited, the spark of knowledge can fan into the flame of passion. So, in essence, by simply picking up this book, you have already taken your first step. The more you learn about the issues, the more you'll find that knowledge can be a surprising impetus to taking action. Read, investigate, ask questions, and pay attention to ways in which your spirit opens up.

Many individuals who have made a difference started, not with the head—with getting educated on the facts—but with the heart. Their hearts were sparked, and this in turn ignited their quest for knowledge. This might be someone who entered a forest and suddenly felt the interconnections between all life. Or it might be a mother who felt helpless watching her child die as a result of exposure to environmental contamination. Take a deep look inside yourself, and explore the possibilities of your untapped passions. In the end, it really doesn't matter whether your motivation comes from the head or the heart, as they are forever intertwined and are both essential in creating change.

THE COURAGE TO ACT

> **The vision must be followed by the venture. It is not enough to stare up the steps; we must step up the stairs.**
>
> —VANCE HAVNER

So, after your interest has been sparked, how do you find the courage to take your actions to the next level? This comes from a lot of self-reflection and can lead to incredible personal growth. With your passion in your back pocket, explore the ways in which you can build upon your strengths to make a difference. Maybe you're good with people and can volunteer on public relations (PR) efforts for a local cause. Perhaps you're an artist and can create banners or signs for protests.

The great thing is that even attributes others may not consider positive can come in handy when trying to make a difference. Qualities once known as "stubborn" and "relentless" are magically transformed into "fearless" and "dedicated."

Another way you can fan the flames of your passion is to learn to redirect your negative emotions toward creating positive change. Anger and frustration, channeled positively, can become an unstoppable energy force. Don't confuse this with directing hostility at others or building upon your existing unhappiness. On the contrary, redirecting negative emotions means using those uncomfortable feelings as fuel to get you off your couch and take action—loving action. Often, when you have an outlet for these kinds of feelings, it's a step toward feeling better about yourself—and when you feel better about yourself, you begin to feel the power within. When your actions are in alignment with your beliefs, the energy synthesized makes anything possible.

THE "FIVE-R" MANTRA

Believe that life is worth living, and your belief will help create the fact.

—WILLIAM JAMES

One of the easiest ways to get started making the difference in our environment is to embrace the "Five-R" mantra: *Respect, Rethink, Reduce, Reuse, Recycle*. It may seem simplistic, but its applications are bountiful.

Respect

The first step to making a change toward a more eco-friendly lifestyle is *Respect.* When you have true respect for the planet, respect for your health, and respect for fellow human beings, it changes the way you view the world and our place in it. Respect naturally gives birth to less destructive habits, which honor all life.

Rethink

The old adage is true: haste does make waste! Take the time to *rethink* your lifestyle and current buying patterns. When shopping, make sure you bring your full attention to the task at hand instead of mindlessly picking familiar items off the shelf. When you purchase or use an item, give thought to where it came from and where it will go when you're done with it. Remember that as a consumer, you have purchasing power, and every single penny is a vote for the planet, the people, the future, and for what you believe in. You wouldn't want to endorse a political candidate without investigating his or her stand on issues and campaign agenda, would you? Once you start rethinking your old ways of consuming, you'll be amazed at how quickly the ability to make more Earth-friendly decisions comes to you.

Reduce

After rethinking your buying habits, it becomes easier to cut out the items that could be harmful to you and the environment. *Reduce* the amount you purchase or use. Reducing the items you use not only diminishes the amount of resources and energy used, it also reduces the waste and pollution created and sends a message to the manufacturers about how we, as consumers, want them to conduct business. If we don't buy it, they won't make it—or more likely, with money at stake, companies would feel pressure to make their products Earth- and people-friendly.

Reuse

Many of us are so accustomed to throwing things away that we've forgotten how to creatively *Reuse* what we already have. It seems unbelievable that people would toss out or recycle glass jars or plastic yogurt containers and then turn around and purchase new storage containers for leftovers. In this day and age, we've also become so far removed from much of the production process that we take for granted what the Earth has sacrificed for our luxuries. We don't have to grow or kill our own food or chop down a living tree to make a hot tub. If we did, we'd probably have a better understanding of why we should get the most out of each product. Many people feel they are doing their part to help the planet because they recycle. Recycling helps, but learning to reuse items is an even more significant contribution because a lot of energy is used and pollution created in the recycling process.

THE FRUGAL ZEALOT

AMY DACYCZYN MADE THE DIFFERENCE

Even though Amy Dacyczyn didn't start reusing aluminum foil, composting her dryer lint, and using tuna fish cans as cookie cutters in order to protect the Earth, many environmentalists think of her as a hero. In 1981, Amy and her husband decided they needed to find new ways to economize so they could buy their fantasy New England farmhouse. By shopping at thrift stores, making her own presents, and finding new uses for egg cartons, frozen juice can lids, plastic milk jugs, and brown paper bags, this thrifty woman was able to save almost $50,000 in seven years—quite a feat considering the family of eight had an income of only $30,000 a year!

Amy Dacyczyn and her family were able to buy their dream home, and in the process, this frugal mother discovered that her daily life had become more satisfying. She learned that she didn't want to live the typical American lifestyle, frantically running between a day care center and a hectic job just so her kids could afford the hottest video games, meals at fast-food restaurants, and designer clothes.

Others were inspired by Dacyczyn, and soon she started *The Tightwad Gazette,* a newsletter dedicated to her economizing tips and simple living. The publication became so popular that now past issues have been published in a successful three-book series. Although Amy's motives were initially economical, her message has received praise by many conservationists because her principles embody the environmental goals of reducing, reusing, and recycling.

Recycle

If an item can't be reused, *Recycle* it. It's the next best thing. Even though the process can use a lot of energy and does create some pollution, it's a much lesser drain on our planet's resources than creating the products from scratch. Recycling also keeps a lot of paper, glass, plastic, and aluminum out of our overflowing landfills.

FACT: ACCORDING TO ONE STUDY, ALMOST 85 PERCENT OF WHAT WE THROW AWAY CAN BE RECYCLED.

BABY STEPS

> **I long to accomplish a great and noble task, but it is my chief duty to accomplish humble tasks as though they were great and noble. The world is moved along, not only by the mighty shoves of its heroes, but also by the aggregate of the tiny pushes of each honest worker.**
>
> —HELEN KELLER

You don't need to save the world in a day, nor do you have to change your lifestyle altogether. If you're feeling intimidated, take baby steps instead of trying to jump the entire staircase at once. *Everything* you do, or don't do, makes the difference—no matter how big or small. If you change only one habit for the better, it still counts! Praise yourself for accomplishments—even the seemingly simple ones. Don't compare your achievements to those of others. Instead, use their stories as a source of inspiration. Shed preconceived notions that caring for the planet is a heavy burden filled with self-sacrifice. Instead, revel in the joy: you have the freedom to choose, the freedom to act, and the freedom to make the difference in our world!

TWO

(In)Disposable Society

We must become the change we want to see.

—MOHANDAS K. GANDHI

WOULD YOU LIKE FLIES WITH THAT?

You're exhausted after a stressful day and don't have a thing in your fridge for dinner. So on your way home you stop at the drive-through window at your local fast-food place and order a burger and a soft drink. You feel a little guilty about the extra calories, but it's cheap, fast, and convenient. While waiting, maybe you listen to the radio or perhaps plan the rest of your evening. After you eat your meal, you toss the containers in the trash and carry on with your night.

This scenario is common for millions of Americans every day. From the beginning of the industrial revolution on through the technological revolution, both the population and the pace of living have grown at a mind-blowing rate. As a result, time has, in essence, become one of the most valuable commodities, and therefore the emphasis on inexpensive, "quickie" solutions and increased productivity is at an all-time high. This wouldn't be such a big problem if we, as consumers, were more aware of how our choices affect the environment and our health and if companies were held more accountable for the results of their production practices.

While idling in the car, waiting for a burger, people are pouring pollution into the air. Millions of acres of rain forests are destroyed each year to make room for cattle to graze so we'll have plenty of patties in fast-food restaurants—and many cultures, plants, and animals are being displaced or killed off in the process. In addition, most beef contains hormones or other potentially harmful substances that were injected into the cows to boost productivity. Additionally, many take-out containers are made from nonbiodegradable materials that take hundreds of years to break down in a landfill. It's the furthest thing from a "happy meal," when you really take time to think about it.

FACT: POLYSTYRENE (STYROFOAM) CAN TAKE ABOUT 500 YEARS TO BREAK DOWN IN THE LANDFILL.

In addition to these damaging effects is the issue of where your money is going. Giving money to a company that supports such practices just reinforces its efforts and allows it to expand and increase rates of production.

This example is not meant to overwhelm you or make you feel you should hang your head in shame for the times you've indulged in a little fast food. It's simply an easy way to demonstrate how one simple act can affect the environment in so many different ways—all around the world. You may think that you don't have the time or energy to change your lifestyle. The thought of giving up—or cutting down on—your favorite luxuries or conveniences may make you want to put down this book before you find out "too much." Maybe it seems impossible to change the policies of such large industries. All of these responses are perfectly natural, but the truth is that once you become educated on products and creative alternatives, making smart, eco-friendly decisions will become second nature.

It's as if you're about to drink a soda with a fly in it. Once you see the insect, the drink loses its appeal and putting it down becomes easy. The same goes for practices that harm our Earth. The more you know about the negative and positive impacts associated with certain products and business practices, the easier it will be to let go of old habits. You'll also discover the empowerment that comes from making conscious choices from the heart. It feels good to make choices that improve our world. Making socially responsible decisions doesn't mean you have to lead a serious life of martyrdom. On the contrary, joyful living grows from the seeds of positive change you plant in your life and in the world around you.

SHOP TILL WE DROP?

> Learn to break the habit of unnecessary possessions—a monkey on everybody's back—but avoid a self-abnegating anti-joyous self-righteousness. Simplicity is light, carefree, neat and loving—not a self-punishing ascetic trip. . . . It is hard to even begin to gauge how much a complication of possessions, the notions of "my and mine," stand between us and a true, clear, liberated way of seeing the world. To live lightly on the earth, to be aware and alive, to be free of egotism, to be in contact with plants and animals, starts with simple concrete acts.
>
> —GARY SNYDER, *TURTLE ISLAND*

Shopping has become the national pastime. We do it because it's fun, and we also do it because we live in a society that is geared to selling us anything and everything. But we don't think about what impact all this getting and spending has on our world. The fact that many production processes that harm the planet are allowed to continue is a direct result of the values we emphasize in our culture.

Health, safety, environmental concerns—and even overall quality of life—are often sacrificed needlessly. We live in a world that so values how we look and what we can buy that we don't focus on the cost to us and our planet of this constant "need" for more. Additionally, advertising and the abundance of new media continue to fuel the fires of consumerism. We are made to feel we aren't good enough if we don't drive the choice car, eat the right cereal, or cover our mouths with the latest shades of lipstick. In turn, we purchase unnecessary products to boost flagging self-esteem or gain social acceptance. This produces more products, which then creates more advertising, and we continue the vicious cycle—purchasing and wasting always more. If "we are what we eat," does that mean we are also represented by what we wear? Yes! But there is more to us than this. We need to see ourselves in a bigger light.

We also get sold on the idea that certain products will help us buy more time by making our lives more efficient when, in actuality, we're just raising the ante on the amount we need to produce, respond to, and act upon within a given period. At the rate we're going, simple living and free time might become as endangered as the Earth.

THE REAL PRICE OF PRODUCTION

Why is it so important to change the way we think about shopping? Because so much is at stake, spiritually and environmentally. Spiritually, if we are valuing ourselves by our possessions, we aren't giving ourselves much of a base upon which to build our lives. Possessions are made to come and go by people who decide what is hot and trendy. Is that the basis for our lives? We are so much more than the sum of what we buy.

Thousands of products, from hair sprays to pesticides to foods to automobiles, have been put on the market before they've been tested thoroughly for their safety on health or the environment. Many of these items are later recalled after consumers discover the harm they can cause. Still, many products with questionable reputations are still available today. This is because we continue to buy them, and there is not a powerful enough force to get harmful items off the market. Our government doesn't test many products for safety, so frequently it's up to the companies themselves to conduct research studies to prove that their own products aren't harmful. Many products that are banned in other major industrialized nations because of lack of adequate studies, have been approved in the United States. Additionally, many companies torture or kill animals in their testing process just so they can produce a razor that "shaves the closest" or a new formula for that "miracle shampoo."

Just paying attention to what we buy is not enough, as globalization is narrowing our options when companies buy other companies, something made much easier by the Free Trade of the Americas Agreement (FTAA), North American Free Trade Agreement (NAFTA), World Trade Organization (WTO), World Bank, and International Monetary Fund (IMF). These new global corporations then wield enormous power and influence. Production and wealth concentrate into fewer and fewer corporate hands, and the public has little to no say in the way these organizations are run. These business officials are not elected by the public and are not responsible to our elected governments. Most of their actions are not even public knowledge. One of the most significant consequences of such organizations is that environmental regulations chosen by the people of one country can now be deemed a barrier to free trade, and that country is bullied into loosening its restrictions or losing business that is critical to its economy. Another result of this global concentration is that these huge companies set up operations in countries where workers are not protected from poor working conditions and where they are paid a pitiful fraction of a fair wage.

If we do not stand up against these institutions by speaking out and holding our government accountable, the option to choose and buy respectfully steadily gets stripped away. Our freedom to choose disappears, as our choices are being made by individuals and institutions that have everything to gain by exploiting or damaging every species, human and otherwise, on this planet. The world desperately needs our help. Your help!

Another reason it's so critical to get a handle on consumption now is the fact that in the past century, the world population has more than tripled and continues to increase exponentially. This means that what we consume and produce creates an even more enormous drain on the planet's resources and produces significantly more waste, resulting in increased pollution to land, water, and air.

TALKING TRASH

We have become a disposable society. Everything must always be new, and everything is thrown away. In no native language are there words equivalent to *waste, disposable,* or *trash*. Deep in our consciousness, we know that everything in our world comes from human beings and resources of the Earth, yet we would never call the planet or one another "waste" or "disposable" or "trash."

FACT: EITHER INDIRECTLY OR DIRECTLY, EACH AMERICAN CITIZEN CONSUMES HIS OR HER OWN BODY WEIGHT IN NATURAL RESOURCES EACH DAY.

The entire situation is compounded because it's really tough giving thought to the future and to the environmental legacy we'll be handing down to future generations. But we are literally stealing from the future and throwing it away. It's not unlike a person who pays no attention to his health until after he's had a heart attack and then starts to watch his diet and exercise. The same thing happens with our Mother Earth. We often ignore the seriousness of her condition until the symptoms become so severe that it becomes difficult or impossible to repair the damage.

Even though it seems like such a large planet, we're creating waste at such a fast pace that we're running out of methods for disposing of all the garbage.

Incinerators to burn the trash only create more pollution, which can lead to asthma and other serious health problems in the neighborhoods where they are located (often in disadvantaged areas and communities of color). Our landfills are at full capacity with trash that isn't biodegradable or can't decompose in the absence of oxygen. The rotting waste creates volatile amounts of methane, which must be vented into the atmosphere, further contributing to global warming. Additionally, one of the primary concerns about landfills is that they often can't be adequately sealed to prevent toxic chemicals from seeping out and poisoning the land, air, and water and the plants, animals, and people in close proximity to it.

THE LOVE CANAL

LOIS GIBBS MADE THE DIFFERENCE

Before 1978, Lois Gibbs may have seemed the most unlikely of heroes. This shy housewife lived with her husband and two children in the district of Niagara Falls, New York, known as the Love Canal. Their lives were fairly quiet until the day Lois read an article in the *Niagara Gazette* about traces of industrial chemicals that had been found in a nearby neighborhood. It didn't take her long to realize that her children's school was built in this area. At the time, her son, Michael, was taking antiseizure medications and suffered from lower-than-normal white blood cell counts, which made him susceptible to infections. Fearing that his medical problems could be related to the toxins, she asked that her kids be moved to another school. The superintendent felt Lois was just being overprotective and denied her request.

With her children's health at stake, this normally introverted mother took a bold stand and started a petition to close the school. Lois began simply by knocking on the doors of each of the residents in the area and educating them on the tainted history of the land where the institution was built. In the 1940s, the Hooker Chemical Company, which produced a range of products—from pesticides to lye—was using the Love

Canal as a chemical disposal site. More than 20,000 tons of waste were buried in large metal barrels in the former canal. In 1953, the board of education bought the land for one single dollar, with the knowledge that the land contained the chemical sludge. Many neighbors Lois talked to were concerned, but others just wanted to look the other way because many people in the community were still employed by the accused chemical copmpany.

Feeling that the state department of health wasn't taking appropriate measures, Gibbs, who had no prior environmental or political experience, wrote to her senators and even consulted a lawyer. She also carpooled to the capitol to attend government meetings on the issue. It was at one such meeting where she heard a report that confirmed her worst fears. The health commissioner stated, "A view of all the available evidence respecting the Love Canal Chemical Waste Landfill has convinced me of a great and immediate peril to the health of the general public residing at or near the site."

When Lois reported back to the residents what she had learned, they immediately formed the Love Canal Homeowners Association and elected Lois Gibbs as president. The grassroots organization earned money with bake sales and raffles. Its inspirational leader hadn't even been to college, and suddenly she was being invited to meetings at the White House to represent hundreds of families. With so much at stake, she also learned how to use the media to get her message across.

Eventually, over four hundred chemicals, including deadly dioxin, were discovered in the area at levels well above safe standards. The Environmental Protection Agency reported that residents in the area were at higher risks for cancer, birth defects, and other health problems. Because of Gibbs's unwavering perseverance, President Jimmy Carter declared a health emergency in the Love Canal district. This meant that the state could buy the contaminated properties from the homeowners (so the residents could afford to move), and it helped many of those affected receive settlements from the Hooker Chemical Company. After winning the bittersweet victory, Lois Gibbs moved to Washington, D.C., and started the Center for Health, Environment, and Justice so she could use her tenacity and newfound passion to lobby Congress on other related environmental issues. This heroic woman showed her community and the world the difference that heart and perseverance can make when seeking positive change.

MAKING THE DIFFERENCE IN YOUR DAILY LIFE

> Judge your success by what you had to give up in order to get it.
>
> —THE DALAI LAMA

Rethink

Differentiate between needs and desires.

Before purchasing a product, think about your motives for buying it. Is it a necessity, or have media messages convinced you that you absolutely need to get it? Is that expensive outfit you just "had to have" now lost in the deep recesses of your closet next to your Chia Pet and retired exercise machine? Try to hold off purchasing something for a few days or a few weeks to find out if your desires stand the test of time, so you aren't spending your hard-earned money on impulsive buys. Remember that the fewer material items you acquire, the more money you'll have to spend on other things, like that trip you've always wanted to take to Bali or those French horn lessons that always seemed too expensive. Living a simpler life might also mean you are able to reduce the amount of hours you work—in essence, buying you more free time.

Research questionable companies.

The Internet makes it quick and easy to find out more about the brands you love. Does the company that manufactures your favorite items have a track record of environmental infractions? Does it exploit workers from less developed nations to get their materials? How does the business's manufacturing process affect the Earth? Does it create pollution, rob the land of scarce resources, or use toxic chemicals? Find out if there are alternative ways to make the product with an environmental conscience. If you can't find answers on the Web, call up a consumer group or the company, letting them know we really do care. With all the facts in hand, you'll be better able to weigh your options and decide which companies you still want to support. (See the "Organizations and Resources" section at the end of the chapter for ideas on where to start such research.)

Learn your labels.

We often assume that a product must be safe or "can't be that bad" if it's on the market, but, unfortunately, this isn't always the case. Learn to decode the often-cryptic labels attached to products. Are the foods you're buying organic, or were pesticides used? Were the cows that produced your milk given growth hormones? Are you feeding your infant genetically engineered baby food? Foods that are not labeled organic under the California Organic Foods Act of 1990 or the Oregon Tilth Organic Food Act often have genetically modified organisms (GMOs) in them, especially if they contain ingredients like soybeans, rice, or corn.

Don't stop there though. Read labels for books, cards, and all paper items you buy. Notice, for example, if toilet paper or feminine hygiene products were bleached with toxic chlorine or are unbleached.

Do you spend more time choosing the scent of your soap than finding out how the ingredients may affect your health or the planet? You wouldn't buy a book if you didn't understand the language written on the back cover, so use the same rule when purchasing foods, medications, and cosmetics, which will eventually end up in our natural environment and inside your and your family's bodies.

Buy recycled.

When you have the choice between purchasing an item made with recycled or nonrecycled materials, try to choose products that use 100 percent post-consumer recycled materials (made completely from used materials). This means that fewer resources and less energy were used when creating this product or its packaging. It also indicates that less ended up in landfill.

Cut out excess packaging.

Don't you hate it when you unwrap a product, only to find the item is half the size it looked with all the packaging? Sometimes the packaging protects items from getting damaged during shipping, but most of the time it's created by an advertising company in the hopes that the fancy wrapping will pop out at you when the product sits next to competitive brands on the shelves. Lots of energy and resources go into the pretty wrapper, which usually ends up in the trash. Choose products with the least amount of packaging. To help reduce the amount of excess waste, buy items in bulk, preferably at places where you can reuse your own containers. Good examples of items to buy in bulk include shampoo, soap, detergents, and food items, including oils, grains, cereals, dried fruits and nuts, and nut butters. Also, consider using alternative packaging when shipping items. Instead of the standard polystyrene packing peanuts, find rice or potato starch versions, or shred used paper for padding.

Just say "no" to chemical pesticides, herbicides, and fertilizers.

When you use chemical pesticides, herbicides, or fertilizers on your lawn or garden or around your house, you are exposing not only yourself but also your kids and pets to harmful chemicals. Additionally, these products drain into our drinking water system as runoff from rainfall. You can have a lush lawn and thriving flowers without the use of such chemicals. Natural manure or compost gives great nutrients to plants. Planting marigolds around your garden can keep out hungry critters. Keeping a good supply of spiders, praying mantises, and ladybugs will also help reduce garden pests. Used soapy dishwater is also a good pesticide for your houseplants.

To prevent ants from colonizing your home, plant spearmint, southernwood, or tansy around the perimeter of your house, or in problem areas indoors, spread chalk dust or chili powder. Combining baking soda with powdered sugar can help get rid of roaches. Boric acid will also do the trick. Putting bay leaves in your cupboards will keep the roaches out. You can also find many organic pesticides and garden products in health or garden stores. Instead of mothballs, use cedar chips, lavender, rosemary, or mint to keep your favorite clothes from being eaten. To keep your pets flea free, add brewer's yeast to their food.

Go green when you clean.

Many advertisers boast that their products will give you the sparkling clean house you see only in commercials. Don't let flashy marketing gimmicks fool you into buying products you don't need and that may be harmful to you and the environment. When you use cleaning products, they're often absorbed into your skin and inhaled into your lungs, and they enter our water supply when they go down the drain. Many safe, organic cleaning products are already on the market, or just use ingredients you may already have around the home. Club soda helps take out stains, orange scents eliminate odors, and baking soda can be used to clean almost anything (mix four teaspoons of baking soda per quart of water for kitchen and bathroom surfaces). Borax (crystalline salt) mixed with water makes a terrific disinfectant. A little vinegar and water in a squirt bottle makes the best window cleaner. Lemon juice mixed with olive oil is great for wood polishing. Use eco-friendly liquid or powdered soap to wash dishes. If you have a dishwasher, use equal parts washing soda (sodium carbonate) and borax. White vinegar and baking soda, followed by boiling water a few minutes later, can help unclog drains.

Steer clear of chlorine.

When chlorine is produced, it creates a by-product known as dioxin, which is very toxic to humans and other living organisms. During the production of chlorine, this chemical can leak into the air, ground, or water and enter your body's system through your lungs, skin, or digestive system. In addition to being classified as a potential carcinogen (cancer-causing substance), it is also shown to cause other major health problems, including liver damage, reproductive problems, rashes, and damage to the nervous system. You'll want to avoid laundry bleach with chlorine as well as paper, toilet tissue, tea bags, coffee filters, and tampons that are bleached with this chemical. If it doesn't say "no chlorine" on the package, chlorine has probably been used. Bleaching processes that use hydrogen peroxide or oxygen are a great alternative. (Find out more about chlorine in chapter 4.)

Hang your old laundry habits out to dry.

As mentioned above, stay away from laundry detergents that contain chlorine. Many alternatives that work just as well but don't use the potentially harmful chemicals are available in health food stores. Additionally, you should avoid typical dry cleaners, as the solutions they use are extremely toxic to the environment. Often, clothes that say "dry clean only" can be hand-washed with a gentle detergent. Also, many green cleaners are popping up all over the country that use Earth-friendly systems to clean your favorite duds. Check your local Yellow Pages to explore your options. And while you're at it, conserve energy by literally hanging your laundry out to dry!

Reuse

Say bye-bye to bottled water.

With the boom in bottled waters, we're creating a lot of excess plastic waste. Many people don't realize that designer waters are often actually just tap water that's been run through a filtering process. Instead of wasting plastic or glass on bottled waters, get a reusable water filter, either a permanent one that you can install in your sink or a portable one that you keep in your fridge. If the H_2O quality in your area can't be trusted, order agua from a reputable delivery service that reuses the jugs when you're finished with them.

FACT: AMERICANS USE AN ESTIMATED 2.5 MILLION PLASTIC BOTTLES EVERY HOUR, OF WHICH ONLY A SMALL PORTION GETS RECYCLED.

Shop for quality instead of convenience.

Many people frequently buy poor-quality, disposable products because they are cheaper or more convenient. You'll actually be saving money in the long run if you purchase long-lasting, durable products that will stand the test of time. For example, buy a metal razor instead of disposable ones, or choose cloth diapers over plastic.

Also stop for a minute and think about why a product is inexpensive. What poor country was deforested to make that table so cheap? How little were the laborers paid, and in what conditions, to bring these grapes to your home in the winter for less than a dollar a pound?

H_2O to go.

Carry your own mug with you everywhere you go (even when you think you won't need it). Use it for the watercooler in the waiting room or that coffee-to-go in the morning or even for drinks in the movie theater!

Value your vessels.

Instead of reaching for the aluminum foil or plastic wrap, save your leftovers in containers, such as glass jam jars or plastic yogurt containers. These reusable containers with lids are great for bringing your lunch to work, for eating out of at picnics, or for transporting take-out foods from restaurants (instead of their over-packaged doggie bags). You can also ditch your cling wrap, as some eco-companies sell reusable plastic covers that resemble shower caps to cover your dishes. Search on-line for this convenient product. To store food, you can also cover your casserole dish with another pan or cookie sheet instead of wasting aluminum foil.

Clean with cloth.

Bring your own cloth napkin to use instead of the paper towels in restrooms. Likewise, use washable rags instead of paper towels to clean up spills around your house. Contrary to popular belief, humans were able to survive and thrive before the creation of these paper products.

Explore the possibilities of paper.

Not only is chlorine used to bleach most paper products, but also tons of trees, water, and energy are wasted in the production process. This is why it's important to reuse the paper we already have. Make sure to use both sides of sheets of paper, or cut it up to create small pieces for notes. If you don't happen to indulge in the art of origami, you can also reuse paper to line your pet's cage or wrap up breakables when packing. An old-fashioned chalkboard is a great alternative to paper for jotting down messages for your family or housemates.

FACT: AMERICANS THROW AWAY ENOUGH OFFICE PAPER EACH YEAR TO CREATE A WALL TWELVE FEET HIGH REACHING FROM LOS ANGELES TO NEW YORK CITY.

Donate the doodads you're done with.

One person's junk is indeed another's treasure! It's amazing how many people throw out clothes, furniture, and other items they don't think they need anymore. Instead, hold a garage sale and donate leftovers to a charitable cause. Your old clothes may provide warmth, or even interview attire, for someone who is homeless or suffering from financial hardships. Your faded sofa may help furnish the new home of a woman who had to flee from an abusive spouse. Likewise, instead of purchasing your wardrobe and home decor from department stores, check out thrift stores and antique shops, or hold a clothing swap with your friends.

Recharge your batteries.

In addition to being nonbiodegradable, batteries also contain chemicals that are very toxic to the environment. It's actually much cheaper in the long run if you purchase a charger and rechargeable batteries. Newer products, including portable stereos, are now equipped with rechargeable batteries and a cord so you can charge them in the machine when it's not in use. As for dead automobile batteries, many auto shops will gladly recycle them for you.

Bring your own bags.

Use cloth shopping bags. Many grocery stores even offer discounts on your purchases when you bring your own bags. Whether to use paper or plastic sacks is a topic that's hotly debated. Plastic doesn't decompose fully, so recycle it. Also, the ink used to print the store logo is often made from cadmium, which is highly toxic when released. The drawbacks with paper bags are the same as with most paper products: we're killing trees, and paper production uses a lot of water and energy as well. Leave a few cloth bags in your car, so that you always have them when you need them.

FACT: IF 25 PERCENT OF AMERICAN FAMILIES USED JUST 10 FEWER PLASTIC BAGS EACH MONTH, AN ESTIMATED 2.5 *BILLION* BAGS COULD BE SAVED FROM LANDFILLS EACH YEAR.

Solve the diaper dilemma.

Disposable diapers cause problems in landfills because they take an estimated five hundred years to decompose. But in addition, they use tons of wood pulp and plastic during their manufacturing. Only a small percentage of parents wash out disposable diapers before throwing them out. This means that millions of tons of possibly virus-infected diapers end up in our supposedly sanitary dump sites. As a result, potentially more than a hundred different viruses that are associated with human feces can seep into our groundwater. By contrast, cloth diapers can be reused at least a hundred times and decompose in a matter of months.

FACT: AMERICANS THROW AWAY ENOUGH DISPOSABLE DIAPERS EACH YEAR TO STRETCH FROM THE MOON AND BACK AT LEAST SEVEN TIMES. (THAT'S NOT A PRETTY PICTURE!)

Make the most of your compost.

Many of us don't think twice about throwing our leaves and grass clippings in the garbage. We think that since it's organic, it must be biodegradable. Unfortunately, in a landfill even organic waste has trouble decomposing, since once it's buried it doesn't receive the oxygen it needs to break down. Instead of throwing your organic food and yard waste in the trash, use it to create nutrient-rich soil for your garden or yard. When making a heap for such a purpose, you should remember to turn the compost with soil regularly so that it's exposed to the much-needed oxygen. Worm composting is also an excellent way to decompose organic waste.

FACT: EVERY YEAR AMERICANS THROW AWAY 28 MILLION TONS OF LEAVES AND YARD TRIMMINGS!

WORMS IN THE "BIG APPLE"

NAOMI DAGEN BLOOM MADE THE DIFFERENCE

Naomi Dagen Bloom lives in New York City and carries around a box of red wiggler worms with her wherever she goes. Tied up in a blue and white polka-dot scarf, this plastic take-out container is her way to kitchen compost on the go. In a city full of colorful individuals, one might think a kinship with these slimy friends must mean she has lost her marbles. On the contrary, this sixty-seven-year-old former psychotherapist has come to her senses about the amount of waste we create and has decided to do something about it. She wants you to bring a compost box into your home.

When Naomi lived in Maryland, she would compost her food and yard waste in her garden. When she retired to an apartment in the "Big Apple," she suddenly realized she was expected to toss the biodegradable materials down the trash chute. Naomi couldn't accept this as a solution, so she would freeze her compost and bring it back to her house in Baltimore for composting. She knew there had to be a better way. Luckily, when she sold the house she found Christine Datz-Romero, who collects composting materials in Manhattan's Union Square Greenmarket. The city had loaned Christine an empty lot, where she installed red wigglers to help her compost food waste brought to her composting table at the market.

These worms instinctively know how to reduce, reuse, and recycle. They break down our food waste into 100 percent organic fertilizer, which invigorates potted plants and New York's very needy street trees. Gardeners pay high prices for this wormy waste, often called "black gold."

Naomi Dagen Bloom was hooked. She bought her own box plus a pound of wigglers. Several times a week she carries out this soothing and rhythmic ritual: she cuts up food preparation leftovers, adds coffee grounds and eggshells, tears up newspaper pages to cover, and sprays with water. Without her own garden, she still can have her hands in the earth.

Naomi also created a performance essay entitled *Composting in New York*, which she performed at any venue that would take her. It became Naomi's mission to educate others about the dire consequences of their actions. Naomi laments, "People are so far removed from the Earth that they don't understand that we can't keep producing and consuming at this rate." *(cont.)*

This worm lover also stages "vermicomposting" (worm composting) demonstrations outside her apartment complex and has influenced a few neighbors to kitchen compost. She enlisted the help of others in making large knitted and crocheted replicas of the worms for an art installation, *This Dirt Museum: The Ladies' Room*. A community-based, interactive three-week show at Queens Botanical Garden, it celebrated a major event for New York City—the closing of Fresh Kills landfill, the largest dump site in the world. The exhibit featured working compost boxes, Naomi's buttons and beads crafted from vermicompost, and photo images of older women glamorously wearing her hand-knitted worms at fancy restaurants.

Naomi's latest scheme is the Worm Wear© Party. Reminiscent of the traditional Tupperware™ or lingerie gatherings, this event features ten remnant-wrapped little boxes just like the one Naomi carries everywhere, complete with ten red wigglers composting within. The boxes are given out to ten lucky guests. On her Web site, www.cityworm.com, many have seen photos of Naomi Dagen Bloom's unusual constant companions enjoying the Great Wall of China, her son's Ph.D. ceremony, and even her daughter's wedding. These amazing creatures are natural conversation starters.

Inquisitive people ask Naomi, "Can the worms survive in your apartment when you travel?" She explains this is why they are perfect pets: they can manage on their own for a couple of weeks. "Since I have a cat, the sitter has always cared for my worms—and become a convert to earth making too!"

When government officials tell Naomi that changing the way cities currently dispose of garbage would just be too expensive, her quick response is, "What's the alternative? Burying ourselves in garbage?" Then she smiles and offers them a copy of Mary Appelhof's best-selling book, *Worms Eat My Garbage*.

Recycle

Recycle paper.

Since the 1950s, over 40 percent of landfill waste has been paper. Recycling, on the other hand, can cut our waste by one-third and saves precious trees and the forest ecosystems dependent on them. It also uses only half as much water and as much as three-quarters of the energy used to produce paper from raw materials. Recycled paper can be used to produce many other products, such as cereal boxes, newspaper, cardboard, tissue paper, and even the paper used in this very book.

FACT: BY RECYCLING ALL OF YOUR NEWSPAPERS FOR ONLY ONE YEAR, YOU COULD SAVE AN ESTIMATED 4 TREES AND 2,200 GALLONS OF WATER AND STOP 15 POUNDS OF POLLUTANTS FROM ENTERING OUR AIR.

FACT: EVERY TON OF RECYCLED PAPER SAVES ALMOST 400 GALLONS OF OIL.

Recycle aluminum and steel cans.

Aluminum cans take a lot of energy to make from scratch. When you recycle soda cans, the energy used and air pollution created is 95 percent less than if cans are produced from raw materials. Steel cans have an outer coating of tin, which is very expensive and must be imported into the United States. This tin can be recovered and resold or used to make new cans. The steel itself is also reusable for other purposes.

FACT: YOU COULD OPERATE A TV SET FOR AN ESTIMATED THREE HOURS WITH THE ENERGY SAVED BY RECYCLING JUST ONE ALUMINUM CAN.

FACT: AMERICANS DISCARD ENOUGH STEEL AND IRON TO CONTINUOUSLY SUPPLY ALL OF THE COUNTRY'S AUTOMAKERS.

Recycle glass jars and bottles.

Glass bottles make up 8 percent of our landfill. Heavier refillable bottles are preferable because they can be cleaned out and recycled up to thirty times. The nonrefillable type can be melted with raw materials to produce new glass bottles.

Recycle plastics.

According to the Environmental Protection Agency, in 1998 plastics made up 10.2 percent (and 24 percent by volume) of our overall waste stream. They also contribute to 6 percent of all litter. Not all plastic can be recycled, which is unfortunate considering it can take hundreds or thousands of years to decompose. Most plastics are currently being made from natural gas and petroleum, but plastics from plant matter that is biodegradable are available and should be more utilized. Current plastic production uses a lot of energy and creates pollution and, often, toxic chemicals.

MAKING THE DIFFERENCE IN YOUR COMMUNITY

We can't live for ourselves alone. Our lives are connected by a thousand invisible threads, and along these sympathetic fibers, our actions run as causes and return to us as results.

—HERMAN MELVILLE

Shop locally.

When you shop at locally owned business, chances are greater that the money will end up being used to help your own community thrive instead of helping some large corporation expand its business and drive out smaller companies. You might also want to look into charitable organizations that donate part of the proceeds from your purchases to environmental and other social causes.

Support local coffee shops, and exercise your influence by demanding they sell organic, shade-grown, fair-trade coffees and teas. If you don't have such a coffee shop in your area, let the other stores know how good, affordable, and rewarding it can be; start your own business; or order such goods on-line. By the same token, do your shopping at locally owned bookstores. They are fast becoming an endangered species. If there isn't one in your area, join with friends and open your own.

Another reason to frequent your neighborhood stores is that you're more likely to know where and how the products were made. The larger corporations are much greater environmental offenders, as they can ravage the Earth of its resources on a much larger scale and at a much faster rate. They can also get away with a lot more infractions because they can afford to pay high lawyer's fees to help get them out of trouble, as well as give financial backing to politicians. Additionally, when you buy from a national or international chain, a lot of pollution is produced by shipping products by land, air, and sea.

Redefine cool.

Develop a new sense of style where everything local, reused, organic, and fair is "hot" and things that come from huge, faraway chain stores are "not." Don't buy into the lie that name-brand clothing makes it, or you, better. Decide that reused clothing is as cool and as important as reused containers and scraps of paper. We need only look at the styles of clothing that go out of fashion only to come back in after a few years to see that we are being conditioned into becoming fine-tuned consumers. Shop at thrift stores. If you do not have one in your area, start one. When you do purchase new clothing, buy hemp, organic cotton, and recycled fibers. Supporting local business also supports individual style, creativity, and vibrant communities—free from the pre-packaged, sterile facades that corporations are using to mass-market to the world. Support local, support beautiful!

Put your money where your mouth is.

Do not buy overprocessed, genetically modified, hormone-filled, and chemically toxic food. Instead, buy local, organic food from a family farm or a community-supported agriculture (CSA) program. Unfortunately, many areas do not currently offer these options, but this is an opportunity to educate ourselves and our neighbors and help build truly healthy communities.

Start community recycling programs.

If your neighborhood, park, office, school, or church doesn't recycle, contact the nearest recycling program to find out how you can start one in your area. Be aware that just because your community doesn't pick up all recycling from the curb, it doesn't mean there aren't drop-off sites nearby. Check with dry cleaners, auto mechanics, supermarkets, manufacturers, and civic organizations to find out where you can take recyclable goods. Also, find out from your employer if your office recycles toner cartridges. If not, find a local business that does printer cartridge recycling, or ask the manufacturer of your current cartridge.

FACT: EVERY YEAR, AMERICANS THROW OUT ENOUGH PRINTER CARTRIDGES TO STRETCH FROM NEW YORK CITY TO LOS ANGELES AND BACK AGAIN.

THE "BEST CITY IN THE WORLD"

JAIME LERNER MADE THE DIFFERENCE

> I think we should have an eco-clock that shows the proportion between saving and wasting. In every city we know the time, the temperature, but we don't have a measure of that city's commitment to the environment.
>
> —*Jaime Lerner*

Imagine a city with clean, tree-lined streets and abundant parks. A place where the poor can trade in their trash for bus tokens or for food from local farms. A commuter's paradise, where buses are always on time and they go as fast as subways, thus decreasing traffic and air pollution. Visualize a community dedicated to human needs and a thriving environment, where residents and business owners work together with the government to make it "The Best City in the World."

At one point, this vision existed only in the mind of a young architect named Jaime Lerner. Because Lerner put his dedication where his heart was, Curitiba, Brazil, has been transformed from a poor, litter-filled town into the incredible model city it is today.

It all started in the 1960s, when Jaime Lerner approached the mayor of Curitiba to express concern over the rapidly growing city. In response, the mayor held a contest and invited the citizens to submit their ideas for a Curitiba master agenda. The mayor then turned the responses over to Lerner and his colleagues to formulate the final plan. In 1971, Jaime became mayor and continued the actualization of this community's collective vision.

Because the economy was poor, Lerner knew he had to start small and cheap and make the process a collaborative effort. Lerner created a visionary recycling program that benefits the people and environment. Citizens are encouraged to separate their organic and nonorganic trash. The organic is given to farmers to use as fertilizer. The poor in the outer areas of town can trade in their trash for food from the local farms or for bus tokens. Poor or disabled employees separate the rest of the garbage collected for recycling. For example, polystyrene products are shredded and used as filler for quilts for the poor. Old unused buses have been refurbished and are now used as classrooms, day care centers, and clinics. Because of Jaime's *(cont.)*

commitment, Curitiba recycles two-thirds of its waste, most of it in a plant built from recycled materials. This system has reduced litter and waste, provided food for low-income citizens, helped farmers, and given jobs to the disabled—and all for the same price as maintaining the landfill!

Of all his incredible achievements, Lerner's most significant was really listening to, and working with, the citizens of Curitiba to cocreate their envisioned community. This inspirational man said it best when he said, "There is no endeavor more noble than the attempt to achieve a collective dream. When a city accepts as a mandate its quality of life; when it respects the people who live in it; when it respects the environment; when it prepares for future generations, the people share the responsibility for that mandate and their environment."

Lerner served three terms as mayor of Curitiba and is now the governor of the state of Parana.

Take litter walks.

Picking up trash while taking walks can be a fun and consciousness-raising activity for the entire family and community. You can clean up your neighborhood or favorite beach while getting some exercise. Just bring along a bag to collect the trash, and wear some protective gloves so you won't get exposed to nasty germs.

Support career-transition programs.

Many laborers continue to work for companies that may have environmentally unsound practices, not because they want to, but because they have families to support. This is why it's so important for communities, including both conservationists and laborers, to work together to create ways in which both the planet and the workers win. Loggers and fisherpeople can be taught sustainable methods or other trades so they aren't dependent on a company and industry that will leave them high and dry once the resources are depleted.

Speak up!

If you think your mechanic should recycle your auto oil, tell him or her. If you don't want a new Wal-Mart in your neighborhood, start a petition. If you don't think the local home supply store should carry lumber from old-growth trees, begin a letter-writing campaign to the company or to your mayor. You'll be surprised at how a community can band together when people have all the facts and the inspiration.

MAKING THE DIFFERENCE GLOBALLY

Think globally, shop locally

One of the largest impacts we have globally is with our money. Buy local. Buy local. Buy local.

Become culture conscious.

To get a better perspective on consumerism and waste, look to other cultures. People from other countries are astounded at the things we throw away. They keep using the same item until it completely falls apart. When taking a resource from nature, people in other parts of the world often use every part of that resource. If an animal is killed for meat, the hide is used for clothing and the bones are used for tools. Nothing goes to waste. In many cultures and religions, such as those of the American Indians and Buddhists, rituals of thanks are given to the animals, plants, and trees that are giving up life to nourish theirs. We could learn a lot about living in harmony with our natural world from those groups whom some might consider primitive.

Ponder the population problem.

Be conscious about the global population crisis when doing your family planning. It is important that we seriously consider "zero population growth" (producing no more than one child per family), and adopting children who need homes and love before producing more offspring.

Share your gripes with the government.

Start letter-writing campaigns to your senators and even the White House officials, letting them know how you feel. Protest the current practices of the Free Trade of the Americas Agreement (FTAA), North American Free Trade Agreement (NAFTA), World Trade Organization (WTO), World Bank, and International Monetary Fund (IMF), which give large corporations the power to exploit the Earth's resources and cheap foreign labor. Let the government know that in order to protect the planet, animals, and people, we need campaign reform so politicians won't let environmental infractions slide because the implicated industries are backing their campaigns. We need to bring the power back to the people, away from the large corporations, which put money before human interest. Our economy can and must thrive without resorting to such means. We need stricter environmental regulations, and these need to be actively enforced. (See the "Organizations and Resources" section on page 42 for addresses for these and other organizations.)

INTERNATIONAL MONETARY FUND

700 19th Street, NW
Washington, DC 20431
Telephone Operator: (202) 623-7000
E-mail: publicaffairs@imf.org

WORLD BANK

Headquarters—General Inquiries
The World Bank
1818 H Street, NW
Washington, DC 20433
Phone: (202) 477-1234
Fax: (202) 477-6391
E-mail: feedback@worldbank.org

WORLD TRADE ORGANIZATION

Centre William Rappard
Rue de Lausanne 154
CH-1211 Geneva 21
Switzerland
Phone: (41-22) 739 51 11
Fax: (41-22) 731 42 06
E-mail: enquiries@wto.org

THE WHITE HOUSE

1600 Pennsylvania Avenue
Washington, DC 20500
Phone: (202) 456-1414
E-mail: president@whitehouse.gov
Web: www.whitehouse.gov

White House Comment Line

To register your opinion on an issue: (202) 456-1111
When bill is signed or vetoed: (202) 456-2226
Vice president: (202) 456-2326 or (202) 456-7125

INSPIRATIONAL ACTIVITIES

- ★ Take a field trip to a factory to see how a product is created.
- ★ Take an outing to a dump site to find out where waste ends up.
- ★ Try limiting yourself to only one bag of trash this month. See if you can reduce your amount throughout the year. You also might want to try to carry all of your

"garbage" around for one day, then one week. It will definitely change the way you look at "disposables."

- ★ Clean your house, and donate unused belongings to a charity.
- ★ Keep a log of all of your purchases for three months.
- ★ Find a new way to reuse a common household item that you would normally throw away.
- ★ Write a letter to an environmentally unsound company, demanding that it take responsibility for its actions.

MEDITATION

I will be caring and conscious in every choice I make. I will live simply and honor all life, striving to live in a way that respects the Earth. I will remember that every living thing on this planet is not waste, disposable, or trash; rather it is sacred, priceless, and precious.

ORGANIZATIONS AND RESOURCES

ADBUSTERS

1243 West 7th Avenue
Vancouver, BC
V6H 1B7 Canada
Phone: (604) 736-9401
Toll-free: (800) 663-1243 (USA and Canada only)
General Inquiries: info@adbusters.org

Adbusters is an ecological magazine dedicated to examining the relationship between human beings and their physical and mental environment. "We want a world in which the economy and ecology resonate in balance. We want folks to get mad about corporate disinformation, injustices in the global economy, and any industry that pollutes our physical or mental commons."

ACTION NETWORK

Web: www.actionnetwork.org

A project of the Environmental Defense Fund, this simple site helps you send faxes and e-mails to members of Congress and other decision makers on behalf of dozens of national and local environmental groups.

CENTER FOR HEALTH, ENVIRONMENT, AND JUSTICE

150 South Washington, Suite 300
PO Box 6806
Falls Church, VA 22040
Phone: (703) 237-2249
E-mail: chej@chej.org

CO-OP AMERICA

1612 K Street, NW, Suite 600
Washington, DC 20006
Phone: (202) 872-5307
Web: www.coopamerica.org

Co-op America helps promote small businesses and lifestyles that are sustainable. This terrific organization publishes an excellent quarterly magazine and an incredible resource guide, *The National Green Pages*.

CORPWATCH

PO Box 29344
San Francisco, CA 94129
Phone: (415) 561-6568
Web: www.corpwatch.org
E-mail: corpwatch@corpwatch.org

CorpWatch is an on-line activism center and on-line magazine for people concerned about the effects of corporate globalization. It's an information clearinghouse, an action tool on issues of corporate accountability.

THE CENTER FOR A LIVABLE FUTURE

Johns Hopkins University
School of Hygiene and Public Health
615 North Wolfe Street, Suite 8503
Baltimore, MD 21205
Web: www.jhsph.edu/environment/index.html

The mission of the Center for a Livable Future is to establish a global resource to develop and disseminate information and to promote policies for the protection of health, the global environment, and our ability to sustain life for future generations.

CONSUMER REPORTS

Consumer Reports
101 Truman Avenue
Yonkers, NY 10703
Web: www.consumerreports.org

Find out which products will stand the test of time by researching them first with consumer organizations such as *Consumer Reports*.

Consumers Union is the advocacy organization that produces *Consumer Reports:* www.consumersunion.org/aboutcu/about.htm

ECOMALL.COM

Web: www.ecomall.com

"Earth's Largest Environmental Shopping Center. Your First Stop to Shop for Green Products That Are Good for People *and* the Environment."

THE GLOBAL DEVELOPMENT AND ENVIRONMENT INSTITUTE

Tufts University
Medford, MA 02155
Web: www.ase.tufts.edu/gdae

Get excellent educational information on sustainable living and the environmental impacts of overconsumption.

GREENMARKETPLACE.COM

Web: www.greenmarketplace.com

A shopping space for people who want to make green choices and want to shop for products that are best for the environment. An on-line store featuring a diverse array of products from tampons to dish soap, all certified "green" by a staff of environmental researchers.

NATIONAL WASTE PREVENTION COALITION

PO Box 24545
Seattle, WA 98124
Phone: (206) 296-4481
Web: www.metrokc.gov/nwpc

Formed by professionals in the solid waste field, the National Waste Prevention Coalition is a clearinghouse for information about ways to decrease our production of solid waste.

THE OFFICE OF SOLID WASTE

US Environmental Protection Agency
1200 Pennsylvania Avenue, NW
Washington, DC 20460
E-mail comments: www.epa.gov/osw/comments.htm

The Office of Solid Waste (OSW) operates under authority of the Resource Conservation and Recovery Act. "We protect human health and the environment by ensuring responsible national management of hazardous and nonhazardous waste. Our goals are: to conserve resources by reducing waste; to prevent future waste disposal problems by writing result-oriented regulations; and to clean up areas where waste may have spilled, leaked, or been improperly disposed of. Individual states adopt federal standards and operate their own waste management programs."

RCRA, SUPERFUND, AND EPCRA CALL CENTER

Phone: (800) 424-9346 or in Washington, DC: (703) 412-9810
TDD: (800) 553-7672 or in Washington, DC: TDD (703) 412-3323

The RCRA, Superfund, and EPCRA Call Center is a publicly accessible service that provides up-to-date information on several of the Environmental Protection Agency's programs. The call center also responds to requests for relevant publications and information resources. You can call the above numbers to speak with information specialists about regulatory questions or to order publications.

REAL GOODS

360 Interlocken Boulevard, Suite 300
Broomfield, CO 80021-3440
Phone: (800) 762-7325
Web: www.realgoods.com

Find products for an ecologically sustainable future.

THREE

We Need a Solution to Air Pollution

No matter how far you have gone on the wrong road, turn back.

—TURKISH PROVERB

If you've ever visited Los Angeles, you've seen what air pollution can do to a city and the surrounding environment. A thick, brownish haze envelops the metropolis and mutes the sunny blue skies. Different levels of smog alerts let the residents know if it's okay to leave their houses on a given day. It may seem like something out of a futuristic sci-fi novel, but it's all too real for the people who live in this region. The scariest part is probably the fact that many have grown so accustomed to living this way that they barely even notice the way the air smells or how hard their lungs have to labor when running.

FACT: AN ESTIMATED 110 MILLION AMERICANS (NEARLY HALF OF OUR ENTIRE POPULATION) LIVE IN AREAS WITH LEVELS OF AIR POLLUTANTS THAT THE FEDERAL GOVERNMENT CONSIDERS HARMFUL.

The problems with smog are compounded by L.A.'s topography (including oceanic air patterns and mountain ranges), which inhibit the polluted particles from dispersing. A main contributor to the air quality problem in this freeway city is the excessive use of private automobiles to go even the shortest distances. This lifestyle came about because Los Angeles, for far too long, has lacked a sufficient public transportation system. In the 1940s, a train system was created, but the auto industry teamed up with tire and oil companies to make sure it didn't flourish. Now the city is desperately trying to undo the damage with stricter emission controls and a new rail system. Unfortunately, it won't be that easy to wean the auto-dependent urbanites off their beloved SUVs, which also double as status symbols. The issue is best demonstrated in one of the many satires about L.A. residents who get in their fancy cars to drive down their driveways to get their mail.

FACT: ON AVERAGE, 140 MILLION CARS IN AMERICA ARE ESTIMATED TO TRAVEL ALMOST 4 BILLION MILES EVERY DAY, AND ACCORDING TO THE DEPARTMENT OF TRANSPORTATION, THEY USE OVER 200 MILLIONS GALLONS OF GAS DOING IT.

FACT: AMERICANS MAKE 123 MILLION CAR TRIPS EACH DAY THAT ARE SHORT ENOUGH TO BE MADE ON FOOT.

Unfortunately, the air pollution problem isn't confined to California. It has reached a critical point in many cities around the world. It's not only individuals driving too frequently that has created an air quality crisis. Many industries that use chemicals in the production of their products, including pesticides, herbicides, and plastics, release toxins into the air, land, and water. Power companies, oil refineries, auto manufacturers, and large cattle companies carry a lot of the blame for emitting exorbitant amounts of carbon dioxide into our environment. Not only have these air pollutants been linked to asthma, lung disease, cancer, and other severe health problems, they are also destroying our planet with acid rain, global warming, and damage to the Earth's protective ozone layer.

FACT: ACCORDING TO THE AMERICAN LUNG ASSOCIATION, AIR POLLUTION IS A KILLER, ACCOUNTING FOR ABOUT 60,000 PREMATURE DEATHS EACH YEAR.

RAIN, RAIN, GO AWAY

So what's the big deal about air pollution? Well, when we burn fossil fuels, such as gasoline or coal, toxic chemicals rise into our atmosphere and form sulfuric acid. This is what causes acid rain. This poisonous rain not only is a health threat to humans, it also kills animals and plants. Additionally, once the pollutants are in an ecosystem, they are impossible to remove. When rain falls into our rivers and oceans, it poisons the fish, which other animals consume. Then, if you eat seafood or meat, you too are ingesting the poison. Vegetarians aren't spared from this vicious food chain either, as plants also absorb the toxins.

A good example of how air pollution can cause a domino effect is seen in the Netherlands. A while back, Dutch scientists were puzzled when they noticed that some bird eggs weren't hatching because the shells were breaking in the nests.

After researching the issue, they eventually zeroed in on the source of the problem. The birds had previously been getting calcium to fortify their eggshells by eating snail shells, which had been receiving their calcium from particles in the soil. Unfortunately, acid rain caused by fossil fuels burned nearby had dissolved much of the calcium content in the soil so that the snails weren't getting their daily intake of minerals. In turn, the nesting birds weren't getting what they needed to make strong shells. If only the snails and the fowls could have banded together to create a "Got Dirt?" marketing campaign, who knows what they could have accomplished!

THE UH-OZONE

Unfortunately, acid rain is only one of the many problems associated with air pollution. The holes in our planet's ozone layer can also be attributed to the very harmful chemicals we've released into the atmosphere. In 1985, scientists discovered that there was a hole over the Antarctic about the size of America! By the year 2000, it had ballooned to more than three times the size of the United States. That year also marked the first time that depletion directly covered populated areas, including parts of Chile and Argentina, as well as the Falkland Islands. This development may be a strong indicator of what lies ahead. We have reason to believe that this depletion has the potential to strongly affect New Zealand, Australia, and even South Africa in the not too distant future.

You don't need to be a scientist to figure out that a hole in our atmosphere can't be a good thing. Ozone is a gas, a form of oxygen, and it lies in a layer about twelve to thirty miles above our planet, buffering us from the ultraviolet rays (UVB) of the sun. Much to Mother Nature's dismay, humans created a family of chemicals called chlorofluorocarbons (CFCs), which interact with sunlight and release chlorine atoms, causing holes in this protective layer. Destruction of the ozone layer increases the amount of harmful ultraviolet radiation reaching the Earth, which can cause increased cases of skin cancer and eye problems such as cataracts. It can also hinder the growth of plants and food crops and is also implicated in the destruction of small organisms, including plankton, shrimp larvae, and young fish. This can cause food shortages all the way up the food chain.

CFCs are widely used in everyday applications, such as coolants for air conditioners, cleaning agents for electronic parts, and in the manufacture of insulating materials and plastics. In 1987, 172 countries ratified the Montreal Protocol on Ozone Depleting Substances, designed to phase out the use of CFCs and other ozone-depleting chemicals. Unfortunately, the protocol has not stopped the deterioration of the ozone layer. Although the plan does phase out the worst ozone-depleting substances (CFCs, HCFCs, halons, and methyl bromide), it allows these chemicals to be replaced with two greenhouse gases, hydrofluorocarbons (HFCs) and perfluorocarbons (PFCs), which contribute to global warming. Both of these chemicals are among the six global warming gases to be controlled under another agreement, the Kyoto Protocol. To date, the American government has done little to protect the ozone layer or enforce the protocols. Washington has failed to support efforts to accelerate the phasing out of HCFCs and has not sufficiently adopted alternatives to ozone-depleting and climate-changing substances. Furthermore, they have come up with every excuse possible to point all of the responsibility for global warming away from American corporations and toward other countries. The Bush administration refused to sign the Kyoto Protocol in 2001 even though the United States is the largest producer of greenhouse gases.

FACT: A SINGLE CHLORINE ATOM CAN DESTROY OVER 100,000 OZONE MOLECULES.

GETTING WARMER

With a better understanding of the ozone layer, you can see how closely the problems are related to global warming. Many of you have probably heard about this phenomenon but may not understand what causes it or realize how serious it is for both the present and our future. The atmosphere that surrounds the Earth allows heat to reach the ground but stops some of it from escaping back out. This is known as the "greenhouse effect." Without this insulating of the atmosphere, it would be so cold on this planet that we would turn into human icicles. As.mentioned in the previous section, global warming is caused by the creation of greenhouse gases. Some of the most damaging include carbon dioxide, nitrogen oxide, and methane. These gases prevent too much of our insulating heat from escaping the atmosphere. It's kind of like being trapped in a car with the heater stuck on "high" and not being able to roll down the windows.

When the temperature of our planet changes, it causes climate transformations that have catastrophic consequences, including unpredictable storms and weather patterns, and floods caused by melting polar ice caps. Such climatic changes also cause severe droughts that make it impossible for farmers to irrigate their sun-scorched crops. These changes in temperature might also kill off some plant and animal species and increase the populations of others, such as mosquitoes and roaches, which thrive in warmer weather.

To make things even more complicated, scientists have learned that while greenhouse gases do cause warming near the ground (the part of the atmosphere called the troposphere), they have an opposite, cooling effect in the upper atmosphere (stratosphere). They trap the heat in the lower atmosphere before it can reach the stratosphere. With the stratosphere cooled, frigid polar air masses develop, forming ice clouds and weather disturbances that further contribute to the destruction of the ozone layer.

So where do these harmful gases come from that contribute to global warming and ozone depletion? Well, a good portion of the methane gas comes from the rotting trash in our landfills. Another major player is the cattle industry. You may have thought it was just a bizarre joke, but cow farts do indeed contribute to global warming. On top of this issue, the slash-and-burn techniques used in deforestation—often done to make room for more cattle grazing—release large amounts of carbon dioxide into our environment. When we cut down trees, we are destroying nature's air purifiers as well. Though all of these factors contribute to the air pollution that is putting our planet in jeopardy, they are far from being the sole causes.

THE POWER PROBLEM

> The United States, Europe . . . and Japan have a habit. They are addicted to heavy energy use, great gulps, and injections of fossil fuel. As fossil-fuel reserves go down, they will take dangerous gambles with the future health of the biosphere (through nuclear power) to keep up their habit.
>
> —GARY SNYDER, *TURTLE ISLAND*

> The power within—the more you give, the more you have to give—will still be our source when coal and oil are long gone, and atoms are left to spin in peace.
>
> —GARY SNYDER, *TURTLE ISLAND*

The main cause of the air pollution that creates global warming is our use of energy. We generate gas and electricity mainly by burning gasoline and petroleum, coal and wood. Both individuals and large industries contribute extensively to our air pollution problem by using excessive amounts of gas and electricity.

Coal is the world's number one energy source, and more than 55 percent of it consumed worldwide is used to generate electricity. The main emissions from coal combustion—sulfur dioxide, nitrogen oxides, and carbon dioxide particulates—make it one of the energy sources most hazardous to our health and the environment. Toxic mercury is also released into the air as a result of the coal burning, and the sulfur dioxide emissions are one of the primary contributors to acid rain. Also, indigenous peoples in places like Big Mountain Arizona are being displaced so that coal can be removed. For these communities, our consumption is destroying their history, culture, and sacred burial grounds, as well as their future.

FIGHTING THE POWER

GREG BOWERS MADE THE DIFFERENCE

For years, Greg Bowers has been fighting to eradicate lethal air pollution created by a coal-burning power plant located south of Seattle, Washington. The aging plant is exempt from modern clean-air regulations because it was built before 1977. According to Bowers, even the Environmental Protection Agency (EPA) and the company running the facility have admitted that there's likely no safe level for the particulate matter that is being emitted by the smokestacks. On top of this, an official with a pollution control agency once called it "the state's single biggest source of air pollution."

In 1995, Bowers, with over twenty years of experience in electrical power planning, began his crusade. The catalyst was the moment when he discovered that an estimated four hundred people each year were dying from the long-term impact of the associated air pollution and that most of those killed had sensitive pulmonary or cardiac systems. Greg Bowers not only testified at the plants' corporate board meetings and meetings with county officials, he eventually used his own money to sue both the company running the plant and the regulatory body that issued a permit allowing the release of 55,000 tons of sulfur dioxide annually. Bower's persistence resulted in a major reduction in sulfur dioxide emissions.

Bowers has paid a huge price for this mission. He's neglected his own business and sold his house and spent almost all of his life savings on living expenses and attorneys. He also likely faces difficulty finding employment in the companies that could most use his services, as they are wary of being sued. But this environmental hero carries on, insisting that industries must be held accountable for their actions. "Does an industry have the right to knowingly cause needless mortalities?" he asks. "I'm not asking the plant to shut down. I'm asking for their economic analysis to include the health costs to people. They'd find cleanup to be justified."

When Bowers is asked why he has dedicated his life to this noble cause, he reports that the EPA estimates that thirty thousand people a year are killed by power plant pollution, but he believes the number to be much higher. "To me, it's like somebody with a gun shooting people. The evidence is that clear," he says. "You're either outraged, or you accept atrocities. We're either going to tolerate industry being allowed to kill, or we're going to fight it."

Burning wood was probably the first energy source, but, unfortunately, it has some of the same drawbacks as coal: it creates a lot of carbon dioxide emissions and harmful particulates. Additionally, new trees may be planted after others are cut down, but their growth rate can't compete with our consumption rate. And when trees are cut down, we are also losing nature's method for removing carbon dioxide from the environment.

SMOKE GETS IN YOUR EYES (AND YOUR LUNGS AND THE ENVIRONMENT)

The majority of the world's population depends on wood as its primary source of energy, particularly in developing countries. In some African countries, wood fuel is the source of 80 percent of the total energy consumed, which emphasizes the importance of forest ecosystems to the survival of the poor. In the United States, only about 3 percent of the total energy consumed comes from wood. Not only does the burning of wood affect our forests and the cultures dependent on them, it also contributes to air pollution, global warming, and serious health problems.

What's more romantic than nestling in front of the fireplace with that special someone, getting cozy, and opening that bottle of wine that you've been saving for the perfect occasion? The scent of wood smoke may stir images of romance, roasting marshmallows, or bonfires on the beach. It can make one misty eyed—even bleary eyed, gasping for breath.

With all the romanticism of wood-burning fires, there is also the fact that burning wood is a major contributor to air pollution, putting people's health at risk. Wood smoke contains hundreds of chemical compounds, such as carbon monoxide and particulate matter. Some of these compounds are known to contribute to cancer. Particulate matter refers to extremely tiny fragments of material given off mostly as smoke. It can come from household fireplaces, wood stoves, forest fires, industries, and automobiles.

These tiny particles can penetrate deeply into the lungs, which can trigger wheezing, coughing, and decreased lung function. It can also bring on asthma attacks in certain individuals. Wood smoke may interfere with proper heart function. Children, pregnant women, people with respiratory ailments, and the elderly are most susceptible to the effects of wood smoke.

Natural gas is a fossil fuel, which has been hailed as a clean alternative to coal and oil because it produces less greenhouse gas. The problem is that, although it is the cleanest of fossil fuels, it is composed mainly of methane, one of the gases linked to global warming. Additionally, since natural gas is a finite resource, the energy industries are always looking for new reservoirs to tap into. This means that pristine areas of scenic beauty are once again threatened with the blight of human industry. Furthermore, the extraction of natural gas is an extremely volatile process, endangering not only the surrounding environment, but also human lives.

The possible consequences, in the case of an accident, could be far worse for the planet, and all life on it, than all the other power sources combined. Nuclear power has many benefits, as it's considered one of the cleaner energy sources and also has a high return of electricity compared with other power generating methods. With all of its attributes, there are major risks for radiation exposure in the event of a meltdown (such as the devastating one in Chernobyl, Ukraine) and in the transporting and disposing of the waste. Even the most fervent proponents of nuclear power probably wouldn't want a plant built in their backyards. The consequences of a nuclear accident are dire: thousands of deaths, cancers, and birth defects in both humans and animals. Even without accidents, there is leakage of the contaminated waste into the environment and people's lives. As always, it is poor communities and indigenous people who have our disrespect dumped at their doorsteps.

The radiation can also travel up the food chain. After Chernobyl, reindeer in Norway ate lichen, which had absorbed the radioactive fallout like a sponge. The radioactivity didn't cause the reindeer noses to glow like Rudolph's, but it did contaminate the reindeer meat, and nobody can tell exactly how many generations it will affect. This is a very important question, since the Saami people of Norway rely on the reindeer for food and income. The jump from the lichen to its effect on human populations didn't take long.

The reindeer example demonstrates how far the wind can carry radioactive particles and the potential chain reactions they can cause. On April 15, 1986, the Associated Press quoted an Environmental Protection Agency warning that "airborne radioactivity from the Chernobyl nuclear accident is now so widespread that it is likely to fall to the ground wherever it rains in the United States." Then only a month later, the AP reported, "An invisible cloud of radioactivity spewed over the Soviet Union and Europe and has worked its way gradually around the world." And on May 17 of that year, the *Minneapolis Star Tribune* observed that "since radiation from the Chernobyl nuclear accident began floating over Minnesota last week, low levels of radiation have been discovered in the raw milk from a Minnesota dairy."

Additionally, since the potential health and environmental risks from nuclear weapons are the same as those from nuclear power, global citizens need to protest the manufacturing and testing of these instruments of destruction as well.

FACT: CHILDREN FROM THE CHERNOBYL AREA WHO SPEND JUST FOUR WEEKS AWAY FROM HOME, EATING UNCONTAMINATED FOOD AND BREATHING UNCONTAMINATED AIR, CAN POTENTIALLY INCREASE THEIR LIFE EXPECTANCY BY TWO YEARS.

MAKING THE DIFFERENCE IN YOUR DAILY LIFE

Power resides in the moment of transition from a past to a new state.

—RALPH WALDO EMERSON

Whenever you save energy, you also reduce the demand for coal, oil, natural gas, and nuclear power. Less burning of these fossil fuels means fewer emissions of carbon dioxide and other air pollutants. There are so many things you can do in your everyday life to improve our planet's air quality and future!

Reduce your auto use.

Walk, bike, skate, scoot, carpool, or use public transportation instead of your own car. If buying a car, consider an electric or hybrid automobile that doesn't rely heavily on gasoline. If you can't afford these types of eco-friendly vehicles, make sure that any car you purchase gets good gas mileage, keep the tires properly inflated, and take it for regular tune-ups. When you have your auto serviced, verify that your mechanics recycle oil, tires, and coolant.

FACT: EACH GALLON OF GAS USED BY A CAR CONTRIBUTES ALMOST 20 POUNDS OF CARBON DIOXIDE TO THE ATMOSPHERE. A SINGLE CAR DRIVING 1,000 MILES A MONTH ADDS UP TO 120 TONS OF CO_2 ANNUALLY.

FACT: IF 190,000 CAR OWNERS STARTED TO GET TUNE-UPS FOR THEIR CARS REGULARLY, IT WOULD KEEP AN ESTIMATED 90 MILLION POUNDS OF CARBON DIOXIDE OUT OF THE ATMOSPHERE.

FACT: IF ALL THE CARS ON U.S. ROADS HAD PROPERLY INFLATED TIRES, IT WOULD SAVE AN ESTIMATED 2 BILLION GALLONS OF GASOLINE A YEAR.

CRUISE CONTROL

JAMES T. BOTSACOS MADE THE DIFFERENCE

For most people, a car salesman is the last person they'd expect to be environmentally conscious. James Botsacos debunks the stereotype of the slick, anything-for-a-buck salesman, as he designed and operates a unique, eco-friendly automobile dealership in Flemington, New Jersey. His store sells hybrid cars that run off both electricity and gas, thus cutting down on air pollution and demand for nonrenewable resources. But that's not all: he also made sure that the planning, design, and construction of his building were done with a deliberate respect for the local environment. The land was minimally disturbed during construction, and the facility was created with pollution prevention in mind. Among its fabulous features is a wastewater system that allows for the recycling of water (until it's sent for treatment) and a glass building design that makes maximum use of natural light, so less heating and lighting are necessary. James Botsacos demonstrates the importance of businesses really rethinking their standard practices and making a conscious decision to tread more lightly on the planet.

Give your house an energy audit.

Ask your local utility company for a home energy audit to find out if your house is energy efficient. Make sure your building is adequately insulated, and use caulk or weather stripping to stop drafts. When replacing windows, opt for the best energy-saving models. You can also get tips for conserving energy from the suppliers of gas and electricity for your home.

FACT: BY INSULATING YOUR CEILINGS AND WALLS, YOU CAN SAVE ABOUT 25 PERCENT IN HOME HEATING BILLS.

Hot stuff . . .

By turning down the heat, Americans could save more than half a million barrels of oil each day! Before reaching for the thermostat, try adding layers of clothes. When you do need to use the heat, you want to keep the temperature at 68 degrees or under. It's also a good idea, when living in colder climates, to paint your house a dark shade and keep air filters and heating vents clean. Only heat or cool rooms you are using, and close vents in unused parts of the house.

FACT: BY TURNING DOWN YOUR CENTRAL HEATING THERMOSTAT ONLY ONE DEGREE, YOUR FUEL CONSUMPTION CAN BE CUT BY AS MUCH AS 10 PERCENT.

Chill out!

Avoid using air conditioners whenever possible. If you just can't beat the heat, try turning your A/C up by a couple of degrees. Cleaning or replacing dirty filters each month could save 5 percent more energy. If you live in a warm climate, you can also keep yourself cool by painting your house a light color and planting trees for shade next to your home.

Hot water fodder.

The hotter the water, the more energy being used. When doing laundry, wash your clothes in warm or cold water, but avoid hot. You can also save electricity by giving your dryer a break and drying your duds on an old-fashioned clothesline. This will also give your clothes a fresh scent you don't have to buy in a box. For cleaning your body, purchase a low-flow showerhead, and try to take shorter showers to use less hot water.

You should also check your hot water heater and make sure the thermostat is between 120 and 130 degrees (or under). This is hot enough to kill bacteria and still save energy. You can also save 7–8 percent of your energy usage by insulating your heater with a prefabricated insulating jacket (making sure you aren't blocking air vents on gas heaters). It's also a good idea to drain two quarts (or two liters) of water from your hot water heater every two months to prevent the accumulation of sediment.

FACT: HOT WATER HEATERS ACCOUNT FOR AN ESTIMATED 20 PERCENT OF ALL ENERGY USED IN U.S. HOMES.

Get enlightened!

One of the easiest ways to save electricity is to become conscious of turning off lights when leaving a room and switching from traditional lightbulbs to energy-efficient ones. If you tend to forget to switch off a particular light, you can put it on a timer so it turns off automatically after a set amount of time. Using a fluorescent lightbulb that doesn't hum or flicker is much more efficient than an incandescent bulb, as it lasts longer and uses about one-quarter of the amount of energy. If we replaced every seventy-five-watt lightbulb with energy-efficient ones, it could prevent one ton of carbon dioxide from entering our environment! By installing a single fluorescent lightbulb in 100 million households in the United States, we would save the energy equivalent to all the energy generated by a nuclear power plant running full-time for one year.

FACT: LIGHTING ACCOUNTS FOR ONE-FIFTH OF THE TOTAL ELECTRICITY CONSUMED BY THE UNITED STATES.

FACT: EVEN THOUGH EFFICIENT FLUORESCENT LIGHTBULBS ARE INITIALLY MORE EXPENSIVE, EACH FLUORESCENT BULB LASTS AN ESTIMATED 13 TIMES AS LONG AS A REGULAR ONE.

Apply energy-efficient appliances.

When purchasing home appliances, choose the ones that are most energy efficient, not the ones that look the coolest. Most dishwashers, washing machines, and refrigerators now have energy guide stickers that tell you how different models rate, based on whether you have a gas or electric water heater. You can consult consumer magazines or Web sites to find out more information. Did you know that by raising the temperature in your refrigerator by ten degrees, you could save 25 percent of your energy? To get your fridge to running more efficiently, clean the condenser coils once a year.

You can also save energy around the kitchen by not keeping the fridge door agape while pondering which snack you want. Save both power and water by running your dishwasher only when you have a full load, and use the energy-saving setting to dry the dishes, let them air dry, or dry by hand.

FACT: AMERICA'S REFRIGERATORS CONSUME 7 PERCENT OF OUR COUNTRY'S ELECTRICITY, WHICH EQUALS THE OUTPUT OF ABOUT 25 LARGE POWER PLANTS.

Buyers, be aware.

Before purchasing products, do your research to make sure nothing you're buying contains CFCs, HCFCs, HFCs, PFCs, or any other chemicals that could be ozone depleting or contribute to global warming. One of the main reasons that aerosol cans containing CFCs were phased out was that many consumers learned about the damages to the ozone and not only voiced their concerns, but also boycotted the harmful products. It didn't mean that people were sweating excessively because they couldn't use their aerosol antiperspirant anymore; they just resorted to new methods, as did the companies who manufactured the containers. It just goes to show, if we don't buy it, they won't make it!

Remember the five R's.

Remember the five R's—Respect, Rethink, Reduce, Reuse, Recycle? These are key for reducing the amount of air pollution caused by the power we waste. Much of the air pollution is caused by the industries manufacturing goods for us to consume. Also, the less we buy, the less waste we have to dispose of, creating a decreased need for incineration and landfill. Recycling is also a significant way to cut down on energy use, as it takes less energy to create many items from recycled materials than from scratch. It's also especially important to recycle your batteries (or preferably use rechargeable ones), as they contain heavy metals, such as mercury and cadmium, which cause air contamination when incinerated and water contamination when put in landfills.

FACT: IF YOU RECYCLE SODA CANS, THE ENERGY USED, AND AIR POLLUTION CREATED, IS 95 PERCENT LESS THAN IF THE CANS WERE PRODUCED FROM RAW MATERIALS.

Cut the cheese.

As mentioned earlier in the chapter, flatulence from cattle and other animals contributes to global warming. This is one of the reasons it's a good idea to cut out or reduce the amount of dairy and other animal products you consume. The more you support these industries through consumption, the more animals they'll breed.

More trees, please!

Plant trees and other greenery. They not only absorb carbon dioxide, they also help produce fresh oxygen!

Use purchasing power.

If you can afford to make the initial investment, purchase solar panels, and get your energy from a plentiful source—the sun! Not only is solar power a clean energy source, the panels can pay for themselves in ten to fifteen years (depending on energy prices) and have an estimated operating life of twenty-five years or more. Regulatory and financial incentives, such as tax credits, grants, low-interest loans, special utility rates, and technical assistance to encourage the installation of solar photovoltaic systems, are available (though they vary from region to region).

FACT: THE SUN PROVIDES ENOUGH ENERGY IN ONE SINGLE MINUTE TO SUPPLY THE ENTIRE WORLD'S ENERGY NEEDS FOR ONE YEAR.

MAKING THE DIFFERENCE IN YOUR COMMUNITY

It's not having been in the dark house, but having left it, that counts.

—THEODORE ROOSEVELT

Promote ride share.

Start a carpool with co-workers or other parents shuttling their little ones between school and activities. Think about piggybacking your errands: when you're going to the grocery store or pharmacy, ask your neighbors if they need you to get anything for them. The fewer cars on the road, the less pollution in the air.

FACT: IF EACH COMMUTER CAR CARRIES ONE MORE PASSENGER, AN ESTIMATED 600,000 GALLONS OF GASOLINE WILL BE SAVED, AND 12 MILLION POUNDS OF CARBON DIOXIDE WILL BE KEPT OUT OF THE AIR.

Work in your jammies.

If there isn't public transportation to your workplace, and it's too far to walk or bike, find out if it would be possible to work from home at least one day a week, thus reducing the number of cars contributing to commuters' pollution and traffic jams.

Shop locally.

Buy food and products that are made in or near your community, to reduce the pollution caused by shipping products by truck, ship, or plane.

FACT: ON AVERAGE, AMERICAN FOOD TRAVELS ABOUT 1,200 MILES FROM THE FARM TO THE CONSUMER.

Spread the word.

Promote energy-efficient measures, and reduce waste in your workplace, church, schools, and community centers. Set up recycling programs where they're lacking. Stress to your co-workers the importance of using less paper and copying or printing on both sides of a document.

Make a power play.

See if businesses, schools, and churches in your region are willing to invest in renewable energy sources, such as bioenergy technologies or solar or wind-powered methods. If such alternative methods are not used in your area, contact utility officials to demand that new systems be adopted.

Do away with diesel.

Demand from your transportation officials that diesel fuel buses be replaced with electric or hybrid methods of public transportation.

BREATHING EASIER

TAMICA DAVIS MADE THE DIFFERENCE

At age thirteen, Tamica Davis was resistant to the idea of interning at an organization that promoted alternatives for the community environment. As you can imagine, plenty of other things sound more appealing to a teenager. Fortunately, Tamica's favorite teacher, Ms. Car, taught environmental studies and encouraged this Roxbury, Boston, youth to give it a try.

During Tamica's internship, she learned that asthma rates in her community were six times higher than the Massachusetts state average. This was attributed to the high levels of air pollution caused by traffic, including that of diesel buses, which spewed out black clouds of smoke when left idling. Tamica felt that it would be next to impossible to get residents to stop driving their cars, so instead she focused on bringing *(cont.)*

awareness to a 1973 anti-idling law, which wasn't being enforced. This tenacious teen decided to organize the Anti-Idling March in memory of a nine-year-old boy who had lived close to the bus terminal and had died from a sudden asthma attack. To bring attention to the event, Tamica made flyers and learned how to give public speeches to educate people on the harmful effects of the diesel buses. She even met with transportation officials, who at first barely gave her the time of day. That would all change.

Tamica persisted because, as she says, "I realized I could do something about the problem and wanted to see how far I could get." Her event was a success! Two to three hundred people, including state officials from the EPA, joined the Anti-Idling March. As a result, the district is now enforcing idling limits, and bus drivers are educated on the topic as part of their training. The transportation authority, which at first ignored Tamica's pleas, pledged not to buy any more diesel buses and is in the process of testing hybrid electric and compressed natural gas forms of transportation.

When asked what older people can learn from her experience, Tamica replies, "If teenagers say that there's something wrong with the world, you should pay attention. Adults need to really listen to the younger generations because we are the future."

JAIME LERNER MADE THE DIFFERENCE

Remember Jaime Lerner, the visionary mayor of Curitiba, Brazil, from the previous chapter? In addition to his incredible recycling efforts, he also saw the same problems Tamica did with the public transportation system. This is why he sat at the bus stops for hours on end and marked down the issues he witnessed. Lerner realized that passengers boarded as slow as molasses because they had to get out their money and feed it into the slot one coin at a time. They were also taking a long time to get on the bus because they had to wait for others to disembark before boarding. All of these things caused the buses to idle for longer periods of time. To combat these problems, Lerner, a former architect, designed new buses for maximum efficiency. Passengers now pay ahead of time in the bus stop area, and they enter and exit through multiple doors on opposite sides of the bus, which significantly reduces the waiting time. These beautiful buses also have their very own traffic lanes and travel as fast as a subway.

Now, nearly two-thirds of Curitiba's population use the public transportation daily, thus cutting down pollution and traffic jams, not to mention irritable passengers. Fuel consumption per head is one-quarter less than the Brazilian average, even though car ownership is the highest in the country. This is the opposite of the normal rule, wherein high ownership usually means high fuel consumption. Curitiba also has one of the lowest levels of ambient air pollution in the country. This is just one more good reason to tip your hat to Jaime Lerner.

MAKING THE DIFFERENCE GLOBALLY

Take into account that great love and great achievements involve great risk.

—THE DALAI LAMA

Encourage auto alternatives.

New carmakers should be taxed based upon their autos' emissions, and that money should go to developing cleaner-burning cars and trains and subsidizing those who ride public transportation. Likewise, the government should enforce stricter emission control standards and create incentive plans for automobile manufacturers to produce cleaner-burning cars. Additionally, oil companies need mandates and incentives to use cleaner fuel without adding toxic chemicals, such as MTBE. Currently ethanol is the better alternative, but the technology exists to make nonpolluting gas. There are actually methods available for creating clean, completely environmentally friendly fuel from our organic waste—biofuel, biogas, or biodiesel.

MAKE WAY FOR THE VEGGIE VAN

JOSHUA TICKELL MADE THE DIFFERENCE

It's called the Veggie Van, and it's fueled with used vegetable oil from fast-food restaurants. During the summers of 1997 and 1998, the Veggie Van and its creator, Joshua Tickell, took America by storm, logging over 25,000 miles on biodiesel fuel. Read Joshua's inspirational account of his amazing journey:

THE VEGGIE VAN IS BORN

During my senior year in college, I cowrote a thesis on energy and the environment with my friend Kaia Roman. Kaia and I often talked about finding a place in the country and living off solar power. As we researched the state of our planet, our dreams began to fade. We learned that global warming, urban sprawl, smog, water pollution, and the need for ever more energy are no longer localized problems. I began to believe that unless people change their energy use and consumption patterns, my children's Earth will be but a shadow of the planet we now call home. I decided to do something radical to bring people's attention to one solution to an environmental problem. The problem we focused on was petroleum use. The solution I wanted to show was vegetable oil.

My goal was to take a Winnebago, paint it with a field of sunflowers, drive it across the country, and fuel it with vegetable oil. Since new vegetable oil from the supermarket is expensive, I would run the motor home on used cooking oil from fast-food restaurants. With Kaia's help, I would turn the fast-food restaurants of America into a network of low-cost gas stations. No sooner had I thought of it than the Veggie Van was born. I found the Veggie Van in a used car lot on the side of the highway in my home state of Louisiana. It was an unimpressive, white 1986 Winnebago LeSharo. It has a small, two-liter diesel engine, and it gets twenty-five miles per gallon.

THE GREEN GREASE MACHINE

Kaia and I approached almost every professor with the Veggie Van idea. Finally, a chemistry professor and a math professor agreed to help us. From then on, support for the Veggie Van project snowballed. The college gave me a garage to work in. Students volunteered to help at all hours of the day and night.

Kaia and I made our first batch of biodiesel in a test tube. Our second batch was made in a blender. Soon, we upgraded to a five-gallon bucket, then to a fifteen-gallon pot. By this time, my 1982 Volkswagen Jetta, "Greasy Gretta," was running on biodiesel made from used vegetable oil we had retrieved from the college cafeteria.

When we were confident making biodiesel on a small scale, I designed a crude processor that could be mounted onto a trailer, which the Veggie Van could tow. My friends and I scavenged boatyards, junkyards, and backyards to find parts for the processor. We found a military steam kettle, a tugboat filter, a champion juicer, an ancient diesel engine from a sailboat, some scrap metal, and some plumbing parts. With these parts, we made a biodiesel processor we called "The Green Grease Machine."

THE VEGGIE VAN USA TOUR

With the help of students and community volunteers, we transformed the Winnebago into a rolling recycling exhibit. Art students painted a Van Gogh–esque field of sunflowers around the Veggie Van. I installed a two-hundred-watt solar power system, and we built the Green Grease Machine. Despite the van's colorful paint job, the only thing we changed about the engine of the Veggie Van was the fuel we poured into it. When we started using biodiesel, the exhaust of the Veggie Van changed from a cloud of black, smelly smoke to a clean, french fry–scented puff of air.

We talked to reporters, environmental organizations, music festival managers, and schoolteachers as we scheduled the events of the Veggie Van Tour and planned our route. We set off on the tour with the Veggie Van, the Green Grease Machine, and an almost endless supply of grease. The Veggie Van traversed more than 10,000 miles of American highways. There was no end to the amount of used cooking oil available to fuel the van. In fact, our greasy voyage did not even make a dent *(cont.)*

in the three billion gallons of used vegetable oil produced annually in the United States.

Life on the American road was a nonstop, colorful adventure. The first question people always asked us was "Does it really run on vegetable oil?" One whiff of the exhaust was enough to convince most skeptics because it does, believe it or not, smell like french fries. During the tour, the Veggie Van was featured on the *Today Show, Dateline NBC,* CNN, the Discovery Channel, and many other news broadcasts. The Associated Press circulated an article about the Veggie Van to newspapers across the country.

POWER TO THE PEOPLE

That summer, Kaia and I talked with farmers who want to run their equipment on oil from the crops that they grow. We found that urban dwellers want public transport without the asphyxiating pollution. We met with CEOs, environmental organizations, and students of all ages who want to study clean technologies. We talked a little, and we listened a lot. We heard the voices of a proud, caring people who love their country, their land, and their air. They want to use clean fuels in their cars and renewable energies in their homes.

By the time the Veggie Van USA Tour ended, it was obvious to me that people care about the environment, and they are ready to work to make a difference. We had received over one thousand e-mails of support and encouragement for the Veggie Van. Many people wanted to make biodiesel fuel themselves. We compiled file cabinets full of biodiesel research with our own experience and wrote a book, *From the Fryer to the Fuel Tank: The Complete Guide to Using Vegetable Oil as an Alternative Fuel.*

As world petroleum reserves continue to decline and energy becomes more expensive, I believe my once-radical dream of living in a house that relies on renewable energy and driving a car that runs on a renewable fuel will become merely a part of everyday life.

—Joshua Tickell, From
"Fueling Around: The Story of the Veggie Van"

Get trained!

We need to let our transportation officials know that we want better public systems that create less air pollution. In countries such as Japan and France, they have high-speed rail systems (the "bullet train" in Japan and TVG in France) that minimize both pollution and use less land. Even more advanced systems, which use magnetic levitation instead of fuel, are in the works.

FACT: TRAVELING AT SPEEDS OF UP TO 300 MILES PER HOUR, EXHAUST-FREE MAGNETIC LEVITATION (MAGLEV) TRAINS COULD HIT THE MARKET AS SOON AS 2005.

Promote positive power.

Many viable alternative energy sources exist that aren't harmful to our planet. We need to let the oil industries and our government know that we won't stand for anything less than renewable, nonpolluting energy sources such as solar- and wind-generated power. We also want more of our tax dollars to be spent on research of bioenergy technologies, which use renewable biomass resources to produce an assortment of energy-related products, including electricity; liquid, solid, and gaseous fuels; chemicals; and heat. Biomass refers to any organic matter available on a renewable basis, including crops, agricultural food and feed crops, agricultural crop wastes and residues, aquatic plants, animal wastes, municipal wastes, and other waste materials. The fuel the Veggie Van runs on is a perfect example of this.

FACT: IN ONE DAY, THE SUN PROVIDES MORE ENERGY THAN OUR CURRENT POPULATION WOULD USE IN ALMOST THIRTY YEARS.

FACT: THE AMOUNT OF SOLAR RADIATION REACHING EARTH IN A THREE-DAY PERIOD IS EQUIVALENT TO THE ENERGY STORED IN ALL OF THE PLANET'S ENERGY SOURCES.

Share your gripes with the government.

We must demand that our government take the threat of global warming and the depletion of the ozone seriously. Stricter air quality standards need to be enforced, and the government should offer companies more incentives to decrease energy and pollution. The United States should support both the Montreal and Kyoto Protocols and make sure that one doesn't undermine the other. Our government also needs to eradicate HCFCs now instead of gradually phasing them out.

INSPIRATIONAL ACTIVITIES

★ Talk to your friends and neighbors about carpooling or piggybacking errands.
★ Bike, walk, or use public transportation for one day. Increase a day each week.
★ Find out if any products you're using contain greenhouse-related ingredients.
★ Plant a tree.

MEDITATION

At the end of a hectic day, take a moment to be still and take a long, deep breath in. Feel it filling up your lungs and then your belly. Imagine that breath going down your legs into your feet. Feel it relaxing all the soreness, stress, and frustration. Let it all go, giving thanks for the gift of air as you release the breath.

With every breath in, I will honor the air that connects all living beings—plants, animals, and humans. With every breath out, I will commit myself to working to protect the quality of air for all life.

ORGANIZATIONS AND RESOURCES

CENTER FOR CLEAN AIR POLICY

444 North Capitol Street, #526
Washington, DC 20001

CLIMATE SOLUTIONS

610 4th Avenue E
Olympia, WA 98501-1113
Phone: (360) 352-1763
Fax: (360) 943-4977
E-mail: info@climatesolutions.org
Web: www.climatesolutions.org

THE ENERGY INFORMATION ADMINISTRATION (EIA)

Specialized Services from NEIC
Energy Information Administration, EI 30
1000 Independence Avenue, SW
Washington, DC 20585
Phone: (202) 586-8800
E-mail: minfoctr@eia.doe.gov
Web: www.eia.doe.gov

GREENPEACE

702 H Street, NW
Washington, DC 20001
Phone: (800) 326-0959
Web: www.greenpeaceusa.org

GREENPEACE INTERNATIONAL

Kiezersgracht 176
1016 DW Amsterdam
The Netherlands
Phone: +31 20 523 6222
Fax: +31 20 523 6200
Web: www.greenpeace.org

NATIONAL CLEAN AIR COALITION

801 Pennsylvania Avenue, SE, Third Floor
Washington, DC 20003

OFFICE OF AIR AND RADIATION

Ariel Rios Building
1200 Pennsylvania Avenue, NW
Washington, DC 20460
Web: www.epa.gov/oar

UNITED NATIONS INDUSTRIAL DEVELOPMENT ORGANIZATION (UNID)

Vienna International Centre
PO Box 300
A-1400 Vienna, Austria
Web: www.unid.org

UNITED NATIONS MULTILATERAL FUND FOR THE IMPLEMENTATION OF THE MONTREAL PROTOCOL

1800 McGill College Avenue
Montreal Trust Building, Montreal
Quebec H3A3JC, Canada
Phone: (514) 282-1122
Fax: (514) 282-0068
E-mail: secretariat@unmfs.org

US ENVIRONMENTAL PROTECTION AGENCY

1200 Pennsylvania Avenue, NW
Washington, DC 20460
E-mail: public-access@epa.gov
Web: www.epa.gov/ebtpages/air.html

THE VEGGIE VAN

E-mail: Tickell@VeggieVan.org
Web: www.veggievan.org

FOUR

Get to Know Your H_2O

Courage is being scared to death and saddling up anyway.

—JOHN WAYNE

Water is so much a part of our daily lives that it's easy for us to take it for granted. We drink it, we clean with it, we water our gardens with it, and we play in it. It supports aquatic life, creates luscious grassy knolls, and quenches our food crops. Water is such a vital life force for our ecosystems, and all life on this planet, that it's imperative that we always be conscious of its gift.

DRINK UP!

The success of the Academy Award–nominated film *Erin Brockovich* got many people thinking for the first time about what mysterious elements might be lurking in their water system. It's amazing how many of us drink this clear liquid from the tap or a bottle without even knowing where it originated. Half of all Americans get their H_2O from underground sources, which can include rainwater and melted snow, and it often contains contaminants that have polluted the ground, rivers, or reservoirs.

FACT: HIGH ABOVE THE ARCTIC CIRCLE, SCIENTISTS HAVE DISCOVERED THAT THE POLAR BEARS IN THIS REMOTE AREA ARE HEAVILY CONTAMINATED WITH INDUSTRIAL CHEMICALS, INCLUDING TOXIC, LONG-LIVED PCBs (A BY-PRODUCT OF PLASTICS).

NOT IN MY BACKYARD!

Many people don't realize that what they spray on their lawns or pour down their drains ends up in our water systems. If you use pesticides or herbicides in your garden, the rainwater can wash it down storm drains or into nearby lakes or rivers, or it can seep into our groundwater supply. The same goes for the chemicals you use to clean your house or do your laundry. What goes down your sink, tub, or toilet is taken to our water and sewage treatment facilities and ends up back in our water system. If you don't want to drink it, don't use it.

Additionally, any toxic substances that aren't disposed of properly, such as paints, solvents, and motor oil dumped on land (even in landfills), in rivers, and down storm drains contaminate our drinking water. This is why it's so important to recycle your oil and contact your community waste facility to find a local drop-off location for such materials.

FACT: ONE QUART OF MOTOR OIL CAN CONTAMINATE UP TO 2 MILLION GALLONS OF FRESHWATER.

OIL, OIL, TOIL, AND TROUBLE

BARBARA BROWN MADE THE DIFFERENCE

Barbara Brown and her two best friends, Kate Klinkerman and Lacy Jones, started the "Don't Be Crude" oil recycling program in Victoria County, Texas. This inspirational act is noble of its own accord, but it takes on more significance when you learn that Barbara and her friends were only in sixth grade when they began their crusade.

After an inspirational science class on water conservation, these youngsters realized that in their rural community, dumping motor oil in one's backyard was more the rule than the exception. Many residents simply weren't aware of what this simple act could do to their underground wells and water supply. The problem was compounded by the fact that there were no facilities in the vicinity for disposing of or recycling the oil. Some residents were even using the oil as a weed killer.

Barbara and her friends first contacted an organization called Still Response, which recycled oil for corporations only. They were then put in touch with the Texas Natural Resource Conservation Commission, which was so moved by the youngsters' cause that it awarded Barbara and her friends a grant to set up recycling centers. The team started with two four-hundred-gallon tanks for collecting the oil, and created promotional "Don't Be Crude" key chains, T-shirts, bumper stickers, and personal oil collection containers—not the kind of gifts your average twelve-year-old girl could appreciate. The trio also met with county commissioners, judges, and businesses to get permission to set up the centers in their community.

On April 18, 1998, Barbara's dream became reality when five centers opened for recycling used oil and hydraulic fluid. Locations included convenient schools and grocery stores. Of the event, Barbara says, "Once the sites opened, farmers and other rural residents seemed to more appreciate the value of natural resources." You might wonder what happens to the used oil once it's been picked up from the centers. It's used to make asphalt for roads!

To keep the program going, these incredible students (or should we say teachers) found five corporate sponsors and are working with a local environmental science teacher to create curriculum plans on crude oil products that correlate with state science standards.

When asked how she stayed motivated, Barbara attributes it to support from their family and friends. She also admits that it felt good to "keep going when people said I couldn't do it. We wanted everyone to see that if even sixth graders can do it, anyone can."

INDUSTRIAL INDISCRETIONS

You probably can guess that individuals aren't responsible for all the water pollution. The agricultural, chlorine,. mining, plastics, and power industries are among the worst contributors to the problem. Most of the water pollution in the United States comes from the runoff from agricultural farms, which use millions of pounds of pesticides and fertilizers every year. These chemicals not only kill aquatic life, they also make their way into our tap water. Once in your system, some of these compounds may end up in your body for life.

About another 10 percent of water pollution comes from industrial dumping. Toxic dioxin from chlorine and PCBs from plastics make up a good portion of this. In recent years, the gasoline additive called MTBE has leaked into a lot of groundwater in the United States. This chemical was initially created to reduce air pollution emissions, which it does, but it's also thought to cause cancer and other serious medical problems in animals and humans—not a great trade-off by any means! Additionally, MTBE is water soluble, so once it's in our water system, it's next to impossible to remove, and it can travel at an incredible pace. Californians had to petition hard for the "right to know," which took shape in the form of a notice put on gasoline pumps that alerted people to the fact that they were being exposed to a carcinogenic substance when pumping gas. Now imagine what such a chemical could do if you were ingesting it! Many states were not as lucky as the Golden State and consumers were never notified about the hidden dangers in their gas. The frightening part of this story is that even after the harmful effects of MTBE came to light, it wasn't banned immediately. Instead, the government is supposed to be phasing it out gradually over several years. Who does our government truly represent by allowing us to be legally poisoned until they decide to phase out harmful chemicals? If governmental officials, or their families, were immediately affected by their choices, don't you think they would get rid of those toxins immediately? They are playing mad scientists and unfortunately we, the innocent, are the experiment.

Many Americans are under the impression that our water and sewage treatment facilities take care of the rest of the pollutants that could end up in our drinking water. It's true that they can filter out some dangerous bacteria and reduce some levels of toxins, but they are unable to remove many hazardous substances. Lime, soda ash, fluorine, chlorine, mercury, arsenic, sulfur, asbestos, pesticides, herbicides, trihalomethane, and lead are just some of the dangerous substances that may end up in your tap water.

One of the primary reasons that our drinking water quality can't be trusted fully is that, once again, politicians are being financially backed by chemical, mining, and oil industries, who benefit from lax environmental standards. The Environment Protection Agency has set standards for more than eighty contaminants that may occur in drinking water and pose a risk to human health. How can any level of a contaminant truly be safe? The EPA says that chronic health effects occur only after people consume a contaminant at levels higher than the safety standards over many years, but how can we be sure? The drinking water contaminants that are classified as having chronic effects are chemicals (including disinfectant by-products, solvents, and pesticides), radionuclides (such as radium), and minerals (like arsenic). Examples of the chronic effects of drinking water contaminants are cancer, liver or kidney problems, and reproductive difficulties. We still don't have a lot of data on how different chemicals and compounds affect pregnant women, children, those with compromised immune systems, or the general public over a lifetime. Do you want to be the guinea pig? Unfortunately, once in our systems, many of these substances never leave, as our bodies weren't designed to break them down.

There is also a debate over adding fluoride to our water. Most people haven't even considered this issue because toothpaste commercials have convinced them that fluoride is essential for a perfect smile and that if dentists recommend it, it must be all right. However, some studies have suggested fluoride can be damaging to your bones and overall health. Would you want strong teeth at the expense of a strong skeleton? Even though the topic is still controversial, either way, shouldn't people have a choice about whether or not they want to be medicated with each glass of water?

THE WATER STREAM MEETS THE BIG SCREEN

ERIN BROCKOVICH MADE THE DIFFERENCE

Many people and animals in the desert town of Hinkley, California, were getting sick. Some had even died. If it weren't for the unwavering persistence and moral outrage of a dyslexic single mother of three, the cause of the mysterious illnesses might never have come out. Erin Brockovich is the perfect example of how you can't tell environmentalists by their Birkenstocks and tie-dyed shirts, as this heroine would be more likely to be found wearing spiked heels and a low-cut, revealing blouse. She couldn't be further from the stereotype of a tree hugger.

Brockovich may not have looked the part and had no prior legal experience when she was hired as an office assistant at the small law firm of Masry and Vititoe, but that didn't stop her from being pivotal in winning an incredible settlement in a civil class action lawsuit. Pacific Gas and Electric, the community's largest employer, had operated a natural gas compressor station in town since the 1950s, and it used a chemical called chromium-6 to keep its pipes from rusting. In late 1987, the utility company reported to the state and Hinkley residents that this chemical had leaked into the groundwater, the town's main water source. PG&E told the community that it would supply them with bottled drinking water. Concurrently, this company also began buying up homes near the plant and destroying them.

Erin Brockovich began looking into the town's water contamination on behalf of a family that didn't want to sell its property. What started as a real estate dispute began to take on a more significant meaning as Brockovich uncovered more and more instances of unexplained medical problems among Hinkley residents, including cancers, respiratory disorders, organ failures, and severe headaches. The levels of chromium-6 in the drinking water were ten times greater than the maximum amount allowed by law. Known as a probable cancer-causing chemical since the 1920s, this chemical is especially dangerous to lungs. Since many of the Hinkley residents were reporting respiratory problems, a link to the contamination seemed highly possible.

As you can imagine, Brockovich's boss, Ed Masry, resisted the idea of going up against one of the largest corporations in America. Erin's persistence and *(cont.)*

mounting evidence finally persuaded Masry to file suit on behalf of 666 Hinkley residents, on the grounds that PG&E had poisoned the town's water with the chemical chromium-6 and had also misled the residents about it. But just as the plaintiffs had experts on their side—experts who said that the chemical had poisoned the community, PG&E had experts who testified that one chemical could not have caused such a large variety of health problems. This is one of the most abominable catch-22s of the chemical industry. Products are being put on the market without sufficient research, and then when they are implicated as the causes for diseases or other medical issues, the cases are dismissed because of insignificant data. It's no wonder that most lawyers wouldn't touch a case such as the one in Hinkley with a ten-foot pole.

Once Masry realized that the lawsuit was much bigger than his little law firm could handle, he joined forces with lawyers from Los Angeles firms that had experience winning environmental-safety cases and also had the financial resources to support such a case. In the end, the plaintiffs offered to submit their claims to binding arbitration, as the case could have dragged on indefinitely, and they might not have seen a potential settlement for decades. It was in PG&E's best interest to take this offer to avoid a potential public-relations disaster if it were to lose.

The arbitrators, each a retired judge, ruled in the plaintiffs' favor, but it was a bittersweet victory. The residents of Hinkley were awarded $333 million, and PG&E was forced to clean up the environment and to stop using chromium-6. In return, the utility company admitted no wrongdoing and no information was released to the public as to the long-term effects of drinking water containing high levels of the chemical.

Fortunately, this is not where the story ends. The case has become a landmark for other plaintiffs whose "preconception" injuries previously would have been completely disregarded. Also, the film based on this true-life case, *Erin Brockovich*, was nominated for a 2001 Academy Award, and actress Julia Roberts won the prestigious Best Actress award for her portrayal of the spunky heroine. Most important, the high-profile nature of the movie brought mainstream awareness to water issues and exposed the potential practices of polluting industries.

Erin Brockovich is now director of research at her law firm. She is bringing more lawsuits against PG&E and represents other groups that have been exposed to chromium in their drinking water.

MINDING THE MINING

Mining near rivers is another great threat to our water and the life living in it. Many mining practices use extremely poisonous compounds, such as mercury and arsenic, to separate metals or minerals from the rock. Mercury contamination not only is an issue in U.S. waters, it also is a huge problem in South America in the Amazon River. Mercury kills the fish, spreads in the roots of trees, harms birds, and also is related to many human deaths. An example of how the mining industry can harm a culture can be seen in the Yanomami Indians. Since 1987, an estimated 15 percent of their population has died as the result of the incursion of Brazilian gold miners and the diseases they carried with them, which the indigenous tribe had little or no resistance against. Another issue with the mining is that the companies are not only harming the water conditions, they are also destroying the natural landscapes and building roads to reach the valuable yet finite resources.

LITTLE WOMAN, BIG MOUNTAIN

YOSEPHA ALOMANG MADE THE DIFFERENCE

Yosepha Alomang may be small in stature, but that hasn't stopped her from going up against the "big boys." The Indonesian province of Irian Jaya, known locally as West Papua, is one of the most biologically diverse places on the planet. It is home to severely at-risk virgin tropical rain forests and the world's largest gold and copper mines, owned by Freeport-McMoRan Copper & Gold, Inc. For years, West Papua's indigenous peoples, including the Amungme, lived a sustainable existence, but more than three decades of mining practices permitted by the Indonesian government have polluted rivers, destroyed rain forests, and displaced communities. Freeport dumps at least 200,000 tons of tailings into local rivers every day, spreading deadly pollutants over vast areas. Meanwhile, Indonesian soldiers repeatedly, often brutally, suppress peaceful protests against the mine. *(cont.)*

In 1994, Amungme community leader Yosepha Alomang was held by police for a week in a room knee-deep with water and human waste, without food or drink. For six weeks she was interrogated for allegedly giving food to Papuan fighters resisting Freeport's land seizures. Because "Mama Yosepha," as she is known, and other leaders continued to speak out fearlessly, these and many other abuses became more widely known. In May 2000, a rock pile at the mine collapsed into a lake sacred to the Amungme, killing four and flooding villages with contaminated water.

Because of this incident, and continued community activism, Indonesia's current government has finally begun examining Freeport's practices. For over twenty years, Mama Yosepha has organized her community to resist Freeport's destruction and the government's complacency. Regardless of danger, her ethnic group has declared independence to gain control over its resources. This fearless woman continues to shepherd projects promoting traditional cultures, collective action, and the well-being of indigenous people in West Papua. Most recently, Mama Yosepha has created a women's group dedicated to environmentalism, human rights, and traditional culture.

WATER (MIS)TREATMENT

Mining and other forms of land development not only cause harm to the water but also can destroy watersheds and wetlands—nature's own water purification systems. A watershed is an area of land that drains into a lake or river. As rainwater and melting snow run downhill, they carry sediment and other materials into our rivers, lakes, wetlands, and groundwater. Watersheds are made up of different layers of porous substances, including rocks, minerals, clay, silt, and sand. Each layer works to filter out toxic substances from the rain and groundwater. If the watershed becomes too full of toxins, its filtration capabilities are severely impaired. Likewise, when too many trees and plants are removed from a watershed area, erosion can occur, which contributes to landslides and the destruction of the purifying system.

Wetlands also have their own self-contained water treatment processes. Organisms living in the water filter out some of the harmful contaminants. Unfortunately, wetlands are extremely fragile, and if one element in the ecosystem is disturbed, it can cause a chain reaction that destroys the entire habitat. Additionally, when watersheds are drained, filled, or converted to agriculture or urban areas, we are also sacrificing a unique habitat that provides flood control and carbon storage. The release of such carbon can contribute significantly to global warming.

FACT: WETLANDS ARE THE SECOND LARGEST STORERS OF CARBON IN THE WORLD.

FACT: HALF OF ALL THE WORLD'S WETLANDS WERE LOST IN THE TWENTIETH CENTURY.

UNDERWATER WORLD

Not only does pollution from industry contaminate our drinking water, it is also responsible for killing many species of plants and animals that live in watersheds, lakes, rivers, and oceans. When an aquatic organism is threatened, an imbalance occurs in the entire ecosystem. A prime example of this is when fertilizers and manure used in agriculture are washed (or dumped) into a river. These nitrates and phosphates act as fertilizer for algae, which grow to harmful levels and kill the freshwater fish and continue out to sea. These algae blooms deplete the water of oxygen, which suffocates the aquatic life and then affects the entire food chain. If a certain plant is no longer available, the organisms that feed on it suffer from starvation. Then other animals that depend on that organism for sustenance also die out. You are most likely to find "dead zones" caused by prolific algae blooms at the point where rivers meet the sea. Sometimes the algae produced is toxic and then all organisms in the area are threatened. Toxic algae blooms are known as "red" tides and can be extremely harmful to the health of humans and the entire ecosystem. As a result of the problems with fertilizers and manure, fisherpeople are often pitted against those in the agriculture industry because their livelihood is being threatened.

Like the fertilizers and sewage waste that contribute to the blooms, many other chemicals, such as dioxins and pesticides, are toxic to river and ocean life and can trigger problems when spread throughout the food chain. A small plant or animal gets poisoned, and then a larger fish eats it and becomes contaminated, and then we ingest the pollutants if we eat that fish.

The aquatic world can also tilt off balance is if a predatory species is killed. Then its natural prey may grow so rapidly that it exhausts its food supply, and other organisms that depend on the same food source starve. This affects the fishing industry, as it competes with other fish and sea mammals for healthy supplies of seafood.

POWER TRIP

Another large adversary to the aquatic world is the power industry. As mentioned previously, air pollution from power plants can contaminate our water sources in the form of acid rain. We also need to look at the long-lasting effects of the *Exxon Valdez* oil spill to see what atrocities are possible when transporting oil or drilling the ocean floor for fuel. Additionally, extraction processes for both oil and gas release toxic chemicals into the water that can harm organisms. On top of these concerns, many power plants near the coast use seawater to cool their turbines, and then, when the water is returned to sea, the high temperatures kill plants and sea animals.

The ocean and its inhabitants can also become contaminated with nuclear waste by illegal dumping, atomic bomb tests, or accidents aboard nuclear-powered vessels or at nuclear reactors located near coastlines. When this happens, the soluble elements dissolve into the sea and the insoluble components of radioactive waste fall to the seabed and affect all marine life.

Many consider hydroelectric dams symbols of human progress. Hoover Dam has even been called one of America's seven modern civil engineering wonders by the American Society of Civil Engineers. Built during the Great Depression of the 1930s, it stands, for many, as a testament to the strength and achievement of the American ideal. Such dams provide hydropower, drinking water, increased agricultural output through irrigation, easier water transport, and flood control. Hydropower is also touted as safe, clean, absolutely renewable, efficient, and affordable. It doesn't emit any atmospheric pollutants or contribute to global warming or acid rain.

Is progress sometimes blinding? Hydroelectric power is not as squeaky clean as once thought. Here's the dirt: For all of their benefits, dams have significant physical impacts on freshwater ecosystems and affect biodiversity, water quality, and food production. Dam building can flood vast amounts of land, alter the amount and quality of water downstream, and affect migratory patterns of fish species. The dams can also collect silt, lowering levels of dissolved oxygen and decreasing the volume of the reservoir, making energy output less efficient. The movement of silt downstream is essential for the fertilization of the river's floodplain. The construction of dams also sometimes poses serious social problems by displacing communities in upstream areas. Additionally, the weight of displaced water has actually tilted our planet on its axis.

FACT: IT IS EXPECTED TO COST ALMOST $8 BILLION TO RESTORE THE FLORIDA EVERGLADES, WHERE A SERIES OF DAMS AND LEVEES HAD CAUSED 68 FISH AND WILDLIFE SPECIES TO BECOME ENDANGERED OR THREATENED WITH EXTINCTION.

THOSE DAMN DAMS!

DAVID BROWER MADE THE DIFFERENCE

We're not just borrowing from our children, we're stealing from them—and it's not even considered to be a crime.

—*David Brower*

It may seem incredible now, but less than forty years ago, our government had a plan to build a dam that would flood the Grand Canyon. The man who was instrumental in stopping this hydropower dam was David Brower, one of the most notable environmentalists of the twentieth century. When Brower found out about the plight of the canyon, the Sierra Club (with Brower at the helm) ran full-page ads in the *New York Times* that asked, "Should we also flood the Sistine Chapel, so tourists can get nearer the ceiling?" This halted the plans for the dam in its tracks.

David Brower often told people he was a graduate of the University of the Colorado River, an institution of higher learning that doesn't issue diplomas and whose classrooms have no walls. From this special place, he learned about the river's cycles, its ebbs and flows and norms and extremes. He uncovered important lessons about human nature, as well as the nature of rivers. From those experiences, he was then able to teach the rest of the world some incredibly valuable knowledge.

Once known as the American Nile, the Colorado River in many places is no longer recognizable. The lower river, once honored for its diverse wetlands, is now a dry salt flat, completely diverted; it no longer reaches the sea or sustains the vital estuary. Yet, despite repeated assaults from dams and development, many sections of this body of water remain the most beautiful of rivers in North America. Next time you visit Dinosaur National Monument or float the Yampa or the Green, thank David Brower that he was able to save those rivers from Echo Park Dam and Split Mountain Dam. You can also appreciate Brower for the fact that the river still runs through Marble Canyon Dam and the Bridge Canyon Dam.

Despite so many environmental successes, Brower still summed up his achievements by saying, "All I did was to slow the rate at which things are getting worse. When they win, it's forever. When we win, it's merely a stay of execution." He lamented his biggest failure, the Glen Canyon Dam on the Colorado River in Utah.

When the dam was completed in 1966, it inundated hundreds of square miles of Utah and Arizona and destroyed some of the most beautiful scenic landscape in the country, not to mention, flooded priceless petroglyphs and pictograms from long disappeared indigenous peoples.

Brower basically traded Glen Canyon to keep the Bureau of Reclamation from creating another dam on the Green River in Dinosaur National Monument, upstream from Glen Canyon. The experience of negotiating away this natural wonder radicalized Brower and made him unwilling to compromise in the future.

While his supporters urged him not to blame himself, he repeatedly reminded whoever would listen that he could have done more to stop what happened to Glen Canyon. He argued that two of his most important lessons were learned at the University of the Colorado River:

1. Never trade away a place you don't know to save a place you care about.
2. Clean up your mess for future generations.

Listening to his own advice, on November 16, 1996, David surprised the world by announcing, "The Sierra Club board supports the draining of the reservoir behind Glen Canyon Dam." David launched a campaign that has only grown ever since. This would be the largest restoration project in history!

Under Brower's energetic leadership of the Sierra Club, 7,000 members grew to over 70,000 by the late 1960s. But by 1969, Brower's radicalism got him kicked out of the Club. That same year he founded Friends of the Earth, the largest environmental group in the world today. He was eventually booted out of this organization, too, but his motto, "Think globally, act locally," lives on. Brower was also the founder of the Earth Island Institute, and it carries on his legacy, supporting the work of numerous groups looking for a better world. One of the organization's exciting programs is the David Brower Youth Awards, which honor young activists.

In his lifetime, David Brower edited more than fifty books. He was nominated twice for the Nobel Peace Prize. He worked to protect more places than most nature enthusiasts visit in a lifetime. His fights embodied more than dams and included crusades for trees, for porpoises, and against pesticides and nuclear power. He took a stand for Americans to prize the natural world beyond its utilitarian value. *(cont.)*

On March 14, 2000, eight months before David passed away, activists in Arizona gathered to hear Brower speak at the International Day of Action Against Dams and for Rivers, Water, and Life. This event was touted as a direct challenge to the hydropower system and was dedicated to a coming century of river restoration, to contrast with the previous century of development and exploitation. David Brower spoke with resolve as he articulated his visions for a restored river to the audience assembled at the site where, only forty years before, had flowed a living river. People listened intently, and many were moved to tears as they realized this might be the last time that David would deliver such a speech.

David passed away on November 5, 2000, not getting to see Glen Canyon restored. He did live long enough to found a movement that will ensure that his vision will be actualized. His call for "CPR"—conservation, preservation, restoration—is gaining momentum around the world.

TOXIC TOURISM

It may seem ironic, but one of the biggest threats to our water life are those who love the water. People who spend their time at the beach or lake often leave their trash around, and it ends up in the water, causing pollution and even the death of the critters that live there. Jet-skis and boats are also large water polluters, leaving trails of gas and oil in their wakes. Additionally, many land developers see big bucks in building hotels and tourist resorts along shorelines, often at the expense of the coral and the inhabitants of the water.

FACT: EACH YEAR, AN ESTIMATED 1 MILLION SEABIRDS AND 100,000 MARINE MAMMALS ARE KILLED AS THE RESULT OF EATING OR BEING STRANGLED BY PLASTIC.

On top of the threat of development, tourism, and mining, coral habitats and plankton are vulnerable to global warming, which is unfortunate considering that under normal conditions plankton and the ocean soak up a lot of the CO_2 that causes global warming in the first place. The catch is that plankton absorbs the most carbon dioxide in cooler waters, yet global warming is causing the water to get warmer. The climate changes caused by global warming are also thought to contribute to excessive bleaching of the coral reefs, which is destructive to the habitat.

Coral reefs are one of the most beautiful and interesting phenomena in the aquatic world. The reef is a rich and colorful community consisting of the coral itself and a variety of plants, fish, and other animals that live on or in it. The base of a reef is formed by the skeleton of dead coral animals, with the living corals and also the algae residing inside the coral giving it color and photosynthetic ability. Healthy reefs, in addition to protecting the inhabitants of the coral, also form a sort of wall to protect the coastal land against brutal ocean waves. Development and global warming threaten coral reefs today, while overfishing and the tourist industry are other major causes of the destruction.

CARING FOR CORAL

BRUNO VAN PETEGHEM MADE THE DIFFERENCE

What started as a battle to stop the development of high-rise buildings on the New Caledonian waterfront turned into Bruno Van Peteghem's crusade to protect one of the world's largest and most unusual coral reefs. New Caledonia is an island in the southwest Pacific, and its geography provides protection from deadly global warming, which is thought to contribute to the bleaching that threatens most coral reefs.

The most serious danger to the reef comes not from towering hotels, but from nickel mining, the island's largest industry. With the support of New Caledonia's dominant ruling party, the Rassemblement pour le Caledonie dans la Republique (RPCR), International Nickel Company of Canada plans to dig up large portions of the reef for calcium carbonate to neutralize its acidic tailings. Numerous other companies are ready to *(cont.)*

proceed with the same process, and New Caledonia has no laws to prevent this catastrophe.

Van Peteghem's campaign to place the reef on UNESCO's World Heritage List is the coral's best hope for protection. He and two organizations he cofounded, the New Caledonian Greens (Les Verts Pacifique) and Living Coral (Corail Vivant), lead a coalition of organizations and indigenous communities to save the reef. Despite serious challenges from the RPCR, key backing for Living Coral has come recently from the leadership of the political party representing the island's indigenous Melanesian people. This is particularly important as Van Peteghem builds the public support that is critical to convincing the RPCR to endorse the World Heritage nomination, which would protect the reefs in perpetuity.

A successful island environmental activist since the early 1990s, Van Peteghem has confronted severe intimidation, death threats, and abuse, including the suspicious burning of his family's home. Asked how he found courage to continue his crusade, this hero said (in his thick French accent), "After the fire, I sat down with my wife and children, and we decided as a family not to give up . . . that we'd always win [when siding] with justice."

GONE FISHIN'

Overfishing is quickly becoming a major problem in many parts of the world. Without a doubt, humans have severely diminished the Earth's fish supply, although there is no consensus about the extent of the damage. Determining the number of fish in the oceans, their ability to withstand fishing demands, and ecological damage is extremely challenging. To complicate matters, fishing must be considered in light of other factors that also affect the marine ecosystem, including pollution, habitat destruction, and environmental changes.

Currently, over 100 million tons of fish are harvested every year. An estimated 37,000 industrial trawlers and 12 million small fishing boats are fishing the world's oceans in this $70 billion-a-year industry. For comparison, industrial ships pull in approximately the same volume of fish annually as the small fishing boats do. Most scientists, and even fisherpeople, now agree that such levels of production are not sustainable. Since 1950, the global fish catch grew more than sixfold to 122 million metric tons in 1997, and the demand for fish for direct consumption is expected to grow another 20 percent by 2010. Maintaining these levels of production is likely to become impossible, with an increasing amount of the burden being placed on fish farming.

FACT: IT IS ESTIMATED THAT IN SOME IMPORTANT FISHERIES, ILLEGAL, UNREPORTED, AND UNREGULATED (IUU) FISHING ACCOUNTS FOR OVER 30 PERCENT OF TOTAL CATCHES.

Even though almost every expert agrees that the oceans are overfished, this threat is barely visible to the general public. Fish meat is readily available at the grocery store, and prices are still relatively reasonable. What most consumers don't know is that the types of fish on the market are not the ones that were on those same shelves ten years ago. Today's fish are the "trash" fish that were once thrown overboard to make room for more "valuable" fish. However, much of the prized fish stocks have vanished, and the throwaway fish of the past have become the catch of the day.

Capture fishing is one of the most common forms of fishing, and it includes every activity that involves catching wild fish or shellfish. Current industrial fishing techniques are much more complicated now than they were in years past, and they are able to swoop up more fish more efficiently and more quickly than previously. The standard industrial ship for capturing fish is the trawler, which may be equipped for harvesting the fish, processing it into fillets, canning or freezing and storing it. These factory ships are often crewed by over five hundred people and can be accompanied by their own fleet of smaller "catcher" boats. It's no wonder that the fish can't reproduce at the rate they are being killed!

Additionally, researchers believe that certain fishing techniques like trawling are capable of destroying entire ecosystems. The trawl works by dragging along the ocean's bottom and scooping up everything in its path, leaving a wake of destruction. Scientists fear that by damaging the ecosystem on the ocean bottom, fisherpeople are desecrating a vital link in the entire marine ecosystem. This type of fishing is slowly tearing apart the ecological system that has been developing for millions of years. There is no way to know how long it could take for the environment to recover.

FACT: AN ESTIMATED 75 PERCENT OF THE WORLD'S MAJOR MARINE FISH STOCKS ARE DEPLETED FROM OVERFISHING OR BEING FISHED AT THEIR BIOLOGICAL LIMIT.

Unfortunately fish farming isn't much better for the environment or our health. Coastal estuaries are destroyed by the excess waste produced and chemicals used. Such farms often use disinfectants to kill bacteria and herbicides to reduce harmful algae and overgrowth caused by the fish waste. The fish are also frequently fed antibiotics and spawning hormones to increase production.

FACT: EACH DAY, AS MANY AS 1,000 DOLPHINS ARE TRAPPED AND DROWN IN FISHING NETS.

FISH OF THE FUTURE?

First came the Bionic Man and the Bionic Woman; now, get ready for Bionic Fish. They may not be able to jump over tall reefs or have X-ray vision to see through coral, but genetically modified fish of the future may contain a hormone to boost their size, an antifreeze protein for increased cold tolerance, and a gene for disease resistance. All joking aside, now that the fishing industry is exhausting its supply, it is looking to genetically modify aquatic species because it sees the potential to increase both the quantity and the quality of products.

These "transgenic" fish may well be on the market within the next few years, and there is concern that this technology poses new risks to the ecosystems and should therefore be carefully regulated to ensure that the environment and human health are not in danger. A contrasting opinion is that such genetically modified organisms (GMOs) are not significantly different from other genetically improved or domesticated species and that they will not survive well in the wild should they escape; therefore, they need no additional testing or monitoring. Unfortunately, there is mounting evidence that shows the opposite. Although no aquatic GMOs are marketed presently, genetically modified soybean is an ingredient of shrimp and other animal feeds that are traded globally, and in turn, genetically modified soybeans can contain fish genes.

ALL ABOUT DROUGHT

Because there are so many oceans and lakes, and because tap water flows readily out of our faucets, we often take water for granted and forget that there can be freshwater shortages with dire consequences. Because of water pollution, acid rain, global warming, hydroelectric power, and overpopulation, it is possible to run out of safe drinking water. Additionally, farmers might not have enough to irrigate their crops during dry spells. When the water tables get too low, it causes desertification (becoming like a desert), which can destroy all habitats that depend on the water source. Even though scenarios in which water becomes more valuable than gold may seem to come straight out of a sci-fi movie like *Dune*, they are a reality in many parts of the world today. For example, the Ogallala aquifier, one of the main water resources for the United States (spanning 225,000 square miles), is dropping frighteningly faster than it is capable of replenishing. Many states and regions of the world can be found fighting over the rights to specific water supplies.

FACT: OF THE 70 PERCENT OF FRESHWATER USED FOR AGRICULTURAL IRRIGATION, ONLY ABOUT 30–60 PERCENT IS RETURNED FOR DOWNSTREAM USE, MAKING IRRIGATION THE LARGEST NEW USER OF FRESHWATER GLOBALLY.

FACT: EVEN THOUGH WATER COVERS TWO-THIRDS OF THE SURFACE OF OUR PLANET, THE FRESHWATER IN RIVERS, LAKES, AND STREAMS REPRESENTS ONLY 0.1 PERCENT OF THE EARTH'S TOTAL WATER.

In addition to polluting our waters, Americans are also wasting huge amounts of water. We take long showers or baths once (or even twice) a day. Gallons more H_2O are lost when we flush our toilets and run our washing machines and dishwashers. Additionally, people don't think twice about ignoring leaky faucets for years on end.

FACT: IN MOST HOUSEHOLDS, ABOUT 40 PERCENT OF THE WATER IS LITERALLY FLUSHED DOWN THE TOILET.

FACT: IF FOUR PEOPLE IN A FAMILY SHOWER EACH DAY FOR FIVE MINUTES, IN ONE WEEK THEY WOULD USE 700 GALLONS OF WATER. THIS IS ENOUGH FOR ONE PERSON TO LIVE OFF OF FOR THREE YEARS.

MAKING THE DIFFERENCE IN YOUR DAILY LIFE

Most of the important things in the world have been accomplished by people who have kept on trying when there seemed to be no hope at all.

—DALE CARNEGIE

Tap into better water.

Remove impurities from your tap water with a portable water filter, or have a permanent one installed by your kitchen sink. Different types of filters are available to screen out pesticides, herbicides, fluorine, bacteria, mercury, lead, and chlorine. Make sure to change the filter cartridge regularly or the system won't work properly. You can also contact your local water utility company to find out exactly what's in your water. Buying bottled water doesn't necessarily mean it's pure. Do your research. If you do buy bottled water, purchase it in bulk, as the process to produce the plastic is highly toxic to water somewhere. Let's be a part of the solution for everyone.

Go with the low-flow.

Save water by taking shorter showers and installing a low-flow showerhead. By purchasing an aerator showerhead, you can reduce the water flow by 50 percent, and the pressure can even feel stronger than with a standard head. Additional agua can be preserved by attaching water-saving devices to the rest of the faucets in your house. You should also remember to turn off the faucet while brushing your teeth.

FACT: A FOUR-PERSON FAMILY TAKING FIVE-MINUTE SHOWERS WITH A LOW-FLOW SHOWERHEAD COULD SAVE AT LEAST 14,000 GALLONS OF WATER A YEAR.

HOW MUCH IS THAT WATER IN THE WINDOW?

OSCAR OLIVERA MADE THE DIFFERENCE

Imagine a place where the citizens are so poor that they can't afford drinking water. In 1999, the Bolivian government responded to structural adjustment policies of the World Bank by privatizing the water system of its third largest city, Cochabamba. The government granted a forty-year concession to run the debt-ridden system to a consortium led by Italian-owned International Water Limited and U.S.-based Bechtel Enterprise Holdings. The consortium also included investment from Bolivia. The newly privatized water company immediately raised prices. With the minimum wage at less than $65 a month for private citizens, many of the poor had monthly water bills of $20 or more. Water collection also required the purchase of permits, which threatened access to water for the poorest citizens.

Oscar Olivera, executive secretary of the Cochabamba Federation of Factory Workers and spokesperson for the Coalition in Defense of Water and Life, known as La Coordinadora, led demands for the water system to stay under local public control. Thousands of citizens protested for weeks. The Bolivian army killed one, injured hundreds, and arrested several coalition leaders. Olivera, who had been forced into hiding, emerged to negotiate with the government.

In April 2000, La Coordinadora won its demands when the government canceled the privatization contract and amended the law that allowed this to happen. La Coordinadora had achieved the first major victory against the global trend of privatizing water resources. Olivera continues to head La Coordinadora's work to develop a water system that relies neither on corrupt government management nor on transnational corporations.

Flush out your water wasting habits.

As mentioned above, a large portion of your clean water is literally being flushed down the toilet. If you can't afford to invest in a new low-flow toilet, there are plenty of inexpensive alternatives. Toilet dams moderate the amount of water being released with each flush. An even cheaper option is to place plastic bottles filled with water or stones in the back of the toilet tank to displace the excess water. Also, many people, who are forced for economic or other reasons to conserve water, choose to flush the toilet only after every few uses. The lid is kept closed in between times. Some may think this sounds "yucky," but remember that many others around the world don't even have the luxury of indoor plumbing. Give it a try and just see if it's possible to "uncondition" yourself. You can also post this conservation motto in your bathroom (frequently used in California during times of drought), "If it's yellow, let it mellow. If it's brown, flush it down."

FACT: PROPONENTS OF WATER CONSERVATION MANDATES SAY THAT LOW-FLOW TOILETS AND SHOWERHEADS CAN SAVE THE AVERAGE HOUSEHOLD ABOUT 30 GALLONS OF WATER EACH DAY.

Don't be a drip.

Do regular inspections of your plumbing to make sure you are not losing water to a pesky leak. You'd be amazed how much water can be lost each year caused by just a little drip.

FACT: IF A FAUCET LEAKS SIXTY DROPS PER MINUTE, YOU COULD WASTE ALMOST TWO HUNDRED GALLONS OF WATER EACH MONTH.

Pool your resources.

As mentioned previously, the chlorine industry (and its by-product, dioxin) is a serious threat to our water supply. If you insist on having a hot tub or swimming pool, invest in an ozone generator, which eliminates the need for superchlorinating while also removing odors, eye irritation and itchy skin, chemical body film, and scum lines. One of the main reasons you don't want to soak in chlorine is the fact that this chemical kills bacteria, which we like when it's bad bacteria. Unfortunately, it also kills the good kinds of bacteria that may keep your body healthy.

Go gray!

Many of us forget that we can use the water that falls from the sky. That's right, rainwater is great for watering plants and flushing toilets. Simply place barrels at the end of your gutter drains, and reap the benefits. You can also save the water you've used to boil food (after it's cool) and the water that normally goes down the drain while you're waiting for it to heat up. Additionally, plumbing systems can be created to collect used water from sinks and showers (not toilets) so that it can be reused. This is known as "gray water."

Guard your yard.

Use only organic fertilizers, pesticides, and herbicides in your household, lawn, and garden. Also, when landscaping, invest in native plants best suited for your local climate.

Recycle your oil.

Recycle your motor oil, and make sure your mechanic does the same. You should never dump oil, grease, antifreeze, pesticides, fertilizers, paints, cleaners, and other toxic household products down the storm drain.

FACT: AMERICANS USE ABOUT 1 BILLION GALLONS OF MOTOR OIL EACH YEAR, AND ABOUT 350 MILLION GALLONS OF IT END UP IN THE ENVIRONMENT. OVER 2 MILLION TONS OF THE OIL ARE DEPOSITED IN OUR RIVERS AND STREAMS ANNUALLY.

Be careful with balloons.

You should never release helium balloons into the air because if they land in the water they can cause the death of countless numbers of fish, sea turtles, and whales. Balloons cause them to suffocate or starve to death by blocking stomach or air valves.

Buy only "Flipper"-friendly tuna and non-endanged fish.

If you can't live without your seafood, reduce the amount you consume. When buying tuna, look for the dolphin-safe label. If purchasing fish, try to find out if organic methods were used in the process.

Don't drain it if you don't want to drink it.

Avoid products manufactured with chlorine. Buy organic toiletries and household cleaning products.

Pay attention at the pump.

When pumping gas, read the posted signs to find out if the gasoline contains dangerous additives like MTBE. Unfortunately, not all states are required to let you know, so you may need to do your own sleuthing, and petition for your "right to know." If the gasoline does contain MTBE, create a fact sheet on the additive to hand out to customers at the gas station.

Revel in responsible recreation.

Build sand castles, go surfing, take a spin in a rowboat, but avoid jet-skis or motorboats because they are huge polluters of both water and air.

Choose your food carefully.

Buy organic foods and, when possible, avoid dairy and beef products, as the excess of cattle creates excess nitrates and phosphates, which get flushed into rivers and eventually into the ocean, killing the fish and other aquatic life.

MAKING THE DIFFERENCE IN YOUR COMMUNITY

Watch your wetlands.

Find out if you have wetlands in your community, and learn what's being done to protect them.

Let it flow.

We aren't beavers, so we don't need to be building dams. Protest any hydroelectric facilities in your region. Advocate for solar energy and the other alternative energy sources that don't cause damage to our waters, to the aquatic life, or displace communities.

INSISTENCE ON TRUTH

MEDHA PATKAR MADE THE DIFFERENCE

> This is not frustration, fear or helplessness, exhaustion or defeat. Nor is it escape from the struggle, rather it is taking the struggle to its height, for the sake of true development. This war will be fought with equanimity instead of hatred, peace instead of violence. . . . We also want to live intensely and with all the joy and beauty of life. We have to bring in the people's rule in this country sans exploitation and oppression; we want to flourish with nature and nature with us.
>
> —*Medha Patkar, 11 July 1999, concluding 8 days silence and fast*

After India gained its independence from Great Britain in 1947, the government wanted to modernize. It followed the examples and the advice of Western countries and development agencies on how a Third World country should develop. Large scale, ambitious plans for dams were made for almost all of the rivers in India. Prime Minister Nehru believed that dams would solve India's water problems, increase agricultural production, and provide energy to growing industries. "Dams are temples of modern India!" he claimed.

Big plans were made for the Narmada River. There would be 30 large dams, 135 medium-sized dams, and 3,000 small dams. Miles and miles of canals would bring water for irrigation to farmers far away. Huge reservoirs would be created to hold drinking water for the large cities, and hydroelectric plants would give the energy necessary to bring India into the modern world. Sounds like a great idea, doesn't it?

Well, this is the largest democracy in the world, so what do the people think? The city people who were promised water and electricity—and were not told of any of the social or environmental costs of the dams—thought it sounded great. But what about the nearly one million people who live in the Narmada River Valley, who could lose their homes, their livelihood and their communities? And what of those countless thousands who could lose their land to the world's largest planned canal system? Are they willing to make that sacrifice?

The Sardar Sarovar Dam was the keystone of the Narmada Valley Development Project. Upon completion, Sardar Sarovar would submerge more than 37,000 hectares of forest and agricultural land. The dam and its associated canal system would also displace some 320,000 villagers, mostly from tribal communities, whose livelihoods depend on these natural resources. They are descendants of the ancient tribes, which settled along the Narmada River valley in prehistoric times. Their ancestors were here long before the Aryan people swept into India around 1500 BCE.

Medha Patkar came to the Narmada River valley as a social worker in the mid-1980s, to learn if the people who were about to be affected by the Sardar Sarovar Dam were being rehabilitated properly. "When we walked through the villages for about two and a half days, and met the villagers . . . it became obvious that the villages were not informed about anything, and no one knew what would be their fate," Medha said. "And they did not know about the project, nor about the rehabilitation. So this was totally unjust. I just made up my mind, the first visit itself, to come here . . . I felt that this was a small replica of the macro issue."

Medha walked from village to village along the Narmada River, informing people of the government's plans and helping them organize themselves. Many of the villages organized into the Narmada Bachao Andolan (or NBA), which means "Save Narmada Coalition." At first the NBA people didn't oppose the dams; they only demanded information on them and on the resettlement programs. When the government refused them information, they gathered it themselves and found that the government statistics were very wrong—from underestimating how many *(cont.)*

people and how much land would be affected, to overestimating how much energy would be produced and how much water would be saved. The Bargi Dam disaster only serves to prove them right.

When the Bargi Dam, the first large dam, was finished in 1985, the government thought that 101 villages would be submerged. When the waters rose, 162 villages were inundated, as the surprised people scrambled to save what they could from their homes. The government had set aside some land for these people, but 22 of these sites were also submerged. Other resettlement sites were either too rocky to farm or had no source of water, or already had people living on them. None of the families displaced by the Bargi Dam has received compensation from the government. The slums of nearby cities are home to these impoverished, landless people. But now there is this dam, right? Can't the people farm all that rich land that is being irrigated by the water from the reservoir? Unfortunately, only five percent of the expected irrigation has been achieved. The cost of the canals wasn't figured into the dam cost. And since construction of the dam already cost almost nine times as much as was expected, there was no money to finish the project.

In 1985, Patkar began mobilizing massive marches and rallies against the Sardar Sarovar project, and, although the protests were peaceful, she was repeatedly beaten and arrested by the police. She almost died during a 22-day hunger strike in 1991.

By 1993, several of the villages were already being submerged by the dam. Supported by their neighbors and activists like Medha, they refused to leave their homes when the monsoons came. They refused to take down their huts or save the posts made from ancient teak trees from their forests. Their animals stayed tied up. The baby remained in his cradle. "We will drowned but we won't leave!" they chanted. And they meant it.

They called this action the monsoon "*satyagraha*." The word *satyagraha*, coined by Mahatma Gandhi, means "insistence on truth." It is a peaceful form of protest, where the protesters refuse to comply with the authorities based on principle. It is hoped that when the government takes action against the peaceful protesters, they will realize that what they are doing is wrong.

Despite government threats and warnings, and despite the very possibility of drowning, Medha and the villagers have insisted that the truth be told and adhered to. The police came in boats and arrested them all, and set their cattle free before the waters could drown them, and the dam continued to be built.

In the years that followed, the struggle grew along with the dam. Thousands of families from over 200 villages made the same vow, that they would not leave their homes. There were rallies and sit-ins, hunger strikes and protests. People have been repeatedly arrested, beaten, and even shot at by the police. One 15-year-old boy from a neighboring village was shot and killed. The police have raped several women known to be active in the resistance movement, with no punishment. But the people have remained peaceful and stand firm.

These actions led to an unprecedented independent review of the dam by the World Bank, which concluded that the project was ill-conceived. Unable to meet the Bank's environmental and resettlement guidelines, the Indian government canceled the final installment of the World Bank's $450 million loan. In 1995, the Supreme Court of India put a temporary hold on further construction while the problems were being worked out. Finally, the people were starting to be heard.

Meanwhile, the sluice gates to the dam were closed, in defiance of court orders, and water was impounded behind the dam.

Unfortunately, in 2000, by a majority of two to one, India's Supreme Court allowed work on the half-finished Sardar Sarovar Dam to continue, rejecting the pleas for an environmental survey to be carried out. The dam was raised 8 meters, including humps that are supposed to slow the water going over the top. That, of course, caused the waters to rise higher, and more villages to be submerged. The *satyagrahas* were resumed. As the water rose, people were arrested again and again, but they just kept returning. Sometimes they would stand up to 36 hours in water up to their waist, or even their neck, as the level of the river rose and fell depending on the rains farther upstream. Finally, when the water level was expected to rise particularly high, 386 *satyagrahis* (people who were participating in the *satyagraha*) were arrested and held for 14 days.

The fight against the Narmada Valley Development project, including the Sardar Sarovar Dam, still continues unceasingly. In addition to protests, vigils, *satyagrahas*, and fasts, the NBA is trying to use India's corrupt court system to stop further destruction. You can read about the most current happenings around the Narmada River at www.narmada.org.

"I will continue to challenge the unjust system that deprives common people, especially the natural resource-based communities who pay the price for the benefit of those who already have much more than them," Medha said in her Supreme Court affidavit. "I will continue to help them raise their voices in protest against this system even if I have to do so against the judiciary and the courts. I will continue to do so as long as I can, even if I have to be punished for contempt for doing that."

—Based on an interview by Judy Abeja Hummel
for www.worldtrek.org

Say no to sea shipping.

Buy locally to avoid the water pollution associated with long-distance shipping.

School your community pool.

Educate your community pool overseers about the benefits of using an ozone generator so that kids and families in your area won't be exposed to superchlorinating.

Opt for organic.

You don't need to wear a straw hat and overalls to support your local organic farms. Buy your produce at organic farmers markets or local health food stores. Help create local organic produce possibilities in communities where there are none!

Join the clean scene.

Find out where to recycle oil and dispose of toxic chemicals in your community. If you don't have a place, start one!

Beautify your beaches.

Organize a day where your community cleans up beaches, rivers, lakes, creeks, and shorelines. It spreads awareness and goodwill. Keep in the know about building developments that could potentially harm your local recreational waters.

MAKING THE DIFFERENCE GLOBALLY

Work toward a sustainable sea.

Let the fishing industries and government officials know we need strong enforcement of sustainable fishing. Currently it appears that the only truly sustainable option is to drastically reduce fishing to let stocks recover before resuming at sustainable levels. We also need more funding for sustainable fishing methods. One way to attain a sustainable system is called polyculture, which means creating a small ecosystem with a variety of species being harvested. Ideally, the populations of the species involved should be arranged so that the many nutrients introduced into the system are recycled among the organisms, thus reducing nutrient pollution and waste, which can contribute to toxic algae growth.

Farm fresh fish.

We need to demand organic certification standards for farmed fish and other seafood. This means no hormones, antibiotics, or herbicides. Additionally, all farms should be moved away from waterways and have strict guidelines for waste management. They should also not be permitted to raise non-native or carnivorous species that could possibly end up in our waters and cause dire imbalances in the food chain.

Respect and protect worldwide waters.

Demand stronger world regulations on fishing practices to prevent overfishing. Governments need to implement measures to stop fishing in vulnerable areas and to crack down on illegal fishing. Plans can be worked out to cycle areas of fishing or limit (through quotas) the number of fish that may be caught. Additionally, governments should provide willing fisherpeople with job transition programs where they are taught sustainable techniques.

Value coral reefs.

Encourage governments to form a global alliance to protect the priceless coral reefs around the world. Protest developments that destroy this precious habitat.

SAVE OUR SURF

JOHN KELLY MADE THE DIFFERENCE

> Humanity flows ahead through powerful systems, changes, and revolutions. Through it all, love and mutual respect for one another, for truth and for nature, remain.
>
> —*John M. Kelly Jr.*

John M. Kelly Jr. may be eighty-three years old, but that doesn't stop him from swimming two hours every day in the ocean surrounding Oahu, Hawaii. And when the swells are right, this famous early big-wave surfer still grabs his board and rides the waves.

Kelly has earned the right to enjoy these waters in his later years, as he spent his life fighting for Hawaii's coastal preservation. "One day in the mid-1960s, when before our eyes, a crane dumped boulders into the sea to destroy a favorite Ala Moana surfing site, the new realism came home. Several of us decided to act. From that decision came 'Save Our Surf,' which has had a measurable impact and been a force in reversing some of the negative historical dynamic of colonization and exploitation. We had some experience in media work, research, trade union organizing. We needed facts to answer the question, 'What's happening?'

"As the answers began to emerge from our search, we realized that to save the threatened shoreline involved pitting ourselves against many of Hawaii's largest corporations, the governor, legislature, and U.S. Army."

As described by Kelly, the SOS strategy rests on three simple concepts: respect the intelligence of the people, get the facts to them, and help the people develop an action program. In 1969, SOS became a strong movement overnight when plans were unveiled by the Army Corps of Engineers and the state to "broaden" the beaches of Waikiki. Members of SOS, mostly teenagers, used old-fashioned political techniques—handbills, demonstrations, and colorful presentations at public meetings—to get their message across:

> To All Planners, Legislators, and Developers: Well, gentlemen—drop your plans! We have prior users' rights in the sea. We swimmers, divers, surfers, bathers, fishermen, conservationists, and park users outnumber you "deci-

sion makers" thousands to one, so please be forewarned: There will be no high rises, no "construction" on the reef at Kewalo.

And:

There will be no parking lot on the Ala Moana Bowl! There will be no more killing of Hawaii's reefs for someone's private profit! No more polluting swimming areas with dredging! No Waikiki at Ala Moana! This entire ocean beach park, from the green grass to the horizon, from the earth to the sky, belongs to the people, now and forever! And this we will defend!

This dynamic movement was instrumental in preserving 140 surfing sites between Pearl Harbor and Koko Head, where hotels, parking lots, and other developments would have destroyed the reef. It was also successful in blocking more than thirty major land developments.

Kelly says, "We learned that our subjective feelings about things were important, an energy crucible, a shared dream or desire to build something. In the beginning, that energy was loose, floating, nearly everywhere, but soft, compliant, unconsolidated, like foaming seas cut by the prow of a ship. We needed a method with which to gather together, aim, and release that energy at the right time and place, like ocean waves that gather their force, rise and break. In SOS, this feeling developed into a basic theme: hang tight on principle, hang loose on implementation!

"We see this theme having wide application. Humanity flows ahead through powerful systems, changes, and revolutions. Through it all, love and mutual respect for one another, for truth, and for nature remain. Some build organizations that hang tight on method but loose on principles, heavily centralize, and rely on hindsight rather than insight. The seas of time inevitably break apart things that are bound too tightly. In SOS, we found from experience that overly tight organization cannot cope with the constant stresses of rapidly changing issues, participants, times, and growth. We believe a flexible style is appropriate for an environmental-political movement of its kind."

This environmental hero also adds, "Early in SOS struggles, we learned that the two principal sides of every conflict had to be thoroughly examined. Issues such as the Waikiki Beach widening or the Kalama Valley evictions are only the surface expressions of deeper contradictory forces. . . . We assess the strengths, weaknesses, motives, capabilities, conflicts, and contradictions of each of the main *(cont.)*

contenders in every struggle—the entrenched propertied wealth of landowners, financiers, developers, etc., and their political agents in government, on the one side, and on the other, the people, the movements, their allied constituencies and internal contradictions."

For his preservation efforts, John M. Kelly Jr. was inducted into the SurfRider Foundation's Environmental Hall of Fame in 1990.

Expect eco-labeling.

All foods, including fish, need to come with eco-labels so consumers know what they're buying and how it was produced. You have the right to know all the facts so you can make educated decisions. Work with consumer and environmental groups to fight for the right to know if products we're using could be dangerous to our water and health. It should be mandated that we're alerted to potential health and environmental effects of anything we buy or consume.

Harvest a new future.

The state and federal government need to provide incentives for farmers and large agribusiness to switch to eco-friendly, organic practices to prevent chemicals and fertilizers from entering our waters. They also need to create alternative methods for irrigation so that we aren't draining our water tables at a faster rate than they are able to replenish.

Share your gripes with the government.

The government should provide incentives for those who participate in sustainable fishing and farming practices. We also don't want our country doing trade with those that are involved in fishing practices that include poaching. Write to the U.S. Fish and Wildlife Service and to the Environmental Protection Agency (addresses following, under "Organizations and Resources").

INSPIRATIONAL ACTIVITIES

- ★ Adopt a sea lion through a marine conservation organization.
- ★ Do a blindfolded taste test of tap and bottled waters.
- ★ Organize a beach, lake, river, or creek cleanup.
- ★ Purchase a water filter.
- ★ Pick up trash along streets so it doesn't go into storm drains.
- ★ Switch to water-saving devices in your home.
- ★ Don't run the water while brushing your teeth.
- ★ Next time it rains, put a bucket outside to see how much water it collects.

MEDITATION

Standing in the shower, feel the water as it flows down your hair, onto your shoulders, curving through your back, and down your legs until it flows away. Be present and aware of how special this gift truly is.

I will honor the life force of water that all of life needs to survive and to thrive, and I will strive to live in a way that protects this sacred gift.

ORGANIZATIONS AND RESOURCES

U.S. FISH AND WILDLIFE SERVICE

Assistant Director—Fisheries
3245 Interior
1849 C Street, NW
Washington, DC 20240
Web: www.fws.gov

ENVIRONMENTAL PROTECTION AGENCY

Ariel Rios Building
1200 Pennsylvania Avenue, NW
Washington, DC 20460
Phone: (202) 260-2090
Web: www.epa.gov/ebtpages/water.html

THE CORAL REEF ALLIANCE

2014 Shattuck Avenue
Berkeley, CA 94704
Phone: (510) 848-0110
Toll-free: (888) CORAL-REEF
Fax: (510) 848-3720
E-mail: info@coral.org

EARTH ISLAND INSTITUTE

300 Broadway, Suite 28
San Francisco, CA 94133
Phone: (415) 788-3666
Fax: (415) 788-7324
Web: www.earthisland.org

INTERNATIONAL RIVERS NETWORK

1847 Berkeley Way
Berkeley, CA 94703
Phone: (510) 848-1155
Fax: (510) 848-1008
E-mail: irn@irn.org

THE OCEAN CONSERVANCY

1725 DeSales Street, NW, Suite 600
Washington, DC 20036
Phone: (202) 429-5609
Fax: (202) 872-0619
E-mail: cmc@dccmc.org
Web: www.oceanconservancy.org

SOIL AND WATER CONSERVATION SOCIETY

7515 Northeast Ankeny Road
Ankeny, IA 50021-9764
Phone: (515) 289-2331
Fax: (515) 289-1227
E-mail: webmaster@swcs.org
Web: www.swcs.org

SURFRIDER FOUNDATION, USA

122 South El Camino Real, #67
San Clemente, CA 92672
Phone: (949) 492-8170
Fax: (949) 492-8142
E-mail: mkremer@surfrider.org
Web: www.surfrider.org

WORLD WATER COUNCIL

Les Docks de la joliette
13002 Marseille
France
Phone: +33 (4) 91 99 41 00
Fax: +33 (4) 91 99 41 01
E-mail: wwc@worldwatercouncil.org
Web: www.worldwatercouncil.org

WESTERN HEMISPHERIC BUREAU, WORLD WATER COUNCIL

Canada
Phone: (514) 286-1050
Fax: (514) 287-9057
E-mail: wwc-yul@worldwatercouncil.org

WATER EDUCATION FOUNDATION

717 K Street, Suite 317
Sacramento, CA 95814
Phone: (916) 444-6240
Web: www.water-ed.org/contact.asp

FIVE

Food (and Fibers) for Thought

> There can be no effective control of corporations while their political activity remains. To put an end to it will be neither a short nor an easy task, but it can be done.
>
> —THEODORE ROOSEVELT

FOOD FIGHT

To be a farmer is a truly noble role. Farmers know that the land is our provider. It gives us our food, our nourishment, our life. The cycle of life and death is played out every time a seed is planted, for it germinates, grows, bears fruit, and dies, only to be born again.

It takes a certain kind of listening to hear the rhythms of the land.

The sound cannot be heard when our listening is tuned into words like *production* and *commodity.* This is what agriculture has become. The official term is *agribusiness.* What is the outcome when the process of life has become twisted into a mechanized, factory-style system of quantified units bought and sold to the highest bidder?

Ecosystems and habitat are destroyed every day under the heavy rumble of the tractor and the cut of the plow. The family farm is a dying tradition. Small and local farmers cannot compete against the financial clout of the large farming corporations.

GARDENING FOR THE SOUL

CATHRINE SNEED MADE THE DIFFERENCE

Cathrine Sneed, a counselor at the San Francisco County Jail, was sure that her home garden had helped her survive a life-threatening illness. She thought the power of the soil might also work on her clients at the jail, mostly drug dealers and users.

Sneed convinced the sheriff to let her create an organic garden on land adjoining the jail. She got prisoners out of their cells to restore an old greenhouse and to clear brambles from the site. At first the Horticulture Project had no tools, so the prisoners yanked blackberries with their bare hands. Sneed begged tools and seeds from local merchants, but she was still short of money, gardening experience, and models for what she wanted to do. The jailers thought she was flaky, especially when she pushed the jail kitchen to serve soothing peppermint tea from the new garden.

But jailer hostility receded as they saw prisoners become enthusiastic gardeners, bringing their zest back to the jailhouse at the end of the day. Some also brought spare seedlings, which they shared with guards, who became home gardeners themselves. Soon there was a waiting list of prisoners eager to join the program.

In short order, the Horticulture Project was harvesting tons of produce a year for the jail, for Project Open Hand (delivering meals to housebound AIDS patients), and for the soup kitchens of Saint Martin de Poores. But the production of food is only a side effect of the project. Sneed says, "We're not just making a pretty little garden here, we're saving lives."

Sneed teaches life lessons from the garden. The prisoners with drug problems see how well the plants grow without chemicals. Many of them have lived on junk food; they see plants flourish with proper nutrients. They discover the taste of fresh vegetables because Sneed cooks lunch for them from the garden. Small farm animals give them experience in nurturing; planning the garden shows the benefits of long-term thinking; and physical labor pays off in visible, edible results. But the most powerful lesson is that mistakes in life, like those in the garden, can be corrected.

Sneed knew that, upon release, her "students" ended up right back in the places where they first got into trouble. A bridge program was needed, so in 1990 she and some former inmates cleared a trash-filled lot near the Bayview housing projects and built the Carroll Street Community Garden. This is the home base of the Garden Project, a combination of counseling, work experience, and job training. Graduates of the jailhouse garden live in two drug-free homes at Carroil Street while they work and train in the garden, go through treatment programs, and attend school. They move on to employment on a third Sneed initiative, the Green Teams, which contract with businesses and the city to do tree planting, gardening, and community cleanups.

Cathrine Sneed points with pride to the rearrest record for her gardeners, which is a quarter that of other former inmates, and to the huge waiting list for her not-flaky-at-all programs. Knowing the power of the gardens to transform both individual and community, she's pushing hard to accommodate the long waiting list of prisoners and to build community gardens in lots all over the city. "I believe in miracles," she says, "but I can't wait for them to just happen."

YOU ARE WHAT YOU EAT

The old adage "you are what you eat" is unfortunately closer to the truth than many people realize. The foods we eat are the foundation of our health. What we ingest can also lead to illness and disease. Many of the pesticides, chemicals, and hormones can stay in our bodies indefinitely, accumulating until we are faced with severe health problems.

Sometimes it's hard to make educated decisions about the foods we buy and eat. To be health conscious means doing your homework. Even the common vegetable, traditionally regarded as wholesome and nutritious, has come under public scrutiny. What does it mean when a vegetable is labeled organic, conventional, genetically modified/engineered, or irradiated? Does it really matter if pesticides are used? Can they simply be washed off? Is there a difference between cows that are fed growth hormones to produce more milk and cows that aren't? And does it matter if the burger you ate came from a cow that was fed antibiotics? Is there harm in any of these practices, or is science actually creating a better product for us, the consumer?

FACT: OVER 100 PESTICIDE INGREDIENTS ARE SUSPECTED OF CAUSING BIRTH DEFECTS, CANCER, AND GENE MUTATIONS.

GROWING PAINS

Civilization began with the birth of agriculture. Food production is a major source of a strong economy. A well-fed society becomes a strong society. But history is also filled with stories of pestilence and famine. In the past, the devastation of crops by pests was considered a natural "act of God." Ruined crops usually meant starvation and death for many.

In the twentieth century, two major forces reshaped agriculture—science and industry. Science has given us an arsenal of weapons to fight the onslaught of pests. When pesticides and fungicides were created, farmers were able to stave off the destructive effects of many insects and molds. New strains of plants were created that could resists pests, drought, and disease. People saw a dramatic increase in food production. Agriculture was moving away from the small farm and toward a mechanized method of farming on a gigantic scale, dramatically increasing output. Food became more plentiful, and living standards rose. With rising living standards, population boomed.

The conventional belief in farming is that switching to organic practices will diminish crop yield. For the last hundred years the use of pesticides and the development of new plant strains have brought us our bounty. After all, aren't we the nation of plenty? How can we just abandon the miracles that science and pure human ingenuity have brought us? The truth is, we don't have to abandon science and human ingenuity. Many scientists and farmers are discovering that it's more profitable in the long run to change the current practices of agriculture.

Just one example of where pesticide usage backfired can be seen in Indonesia in the 1980s. The government encouraged farmers to use more pesticides to kill off the brown planthopper, which was eating the rice plants. Unfortunately, the insect developed an immunity to the insecticides and began to multiply because all of its natural predators had been killed off by the chemicals. The crops were devastated.

Pesticides and herbicides reduce soil nutrients as well as kill all the beneficial organisms in the soil. What you end up with is dead dirt, or soil that is infertile, barren, and unusable for growing. Ironically, many of the weeds that farmers kill off can be used to protect the crops and nutrients by holding the soil in place with their root systems. With the weeds gone, there is nothing to keep the nutrient-rich topsoil from blowing away. This is what created America's infamous Dust Bowl of the 1930s. Unfortunately, once the chemicals are in the land, they are difficult to remove. Likewise, when crops are sprayed, the wind can carry particles of pesticides hundreds of miles.

Some of the pesticides in use today were originally developed to kill human beings in chemical warfare. Many of them are part of the nerve gas family, a poison gas that was heavily used during World War I. Pesticides are a serious threat to human health and the health of other animals. Most people think that you can simply wash the pesticides off the produce, when in fact many pesticides are absorbed into the plant itself.

Pesticides have been linked to many types of cancer in humans. Some of the most prevalent forms are leukemia and lymphoma as well as brain, breast, ovarian, prostate, bone, testicular, and liver cancer. We are just discovering how pesticides disrupt the endocrine system. A dysfunctional endocrine system can play havoc with the complex regulation of hormones, the reproductive system, and embryonic development. Endocrine disruption can produce birth defects, infertility, and developmental defects in offspring, including hormonal imbalance and incomplete sexual development, behavioral disorders, impaired brain development, and many others.

FACT: 40 PERCENT OF ALL PESTICIDES USED IN AMERICAN AGRICULTURE IN 1992 WERE KNOWN ENDOCRINE DISRUPTERS.

FACT: OF THE 35,000 PESTICIDES INTRODUCED SINCE 1945, ONLY ABOUT 10 PERCENT HAVE BEEN TESTED FOR THEIR EFFECTS ON HUMANS.

Rain and irrigation wash pesticides and chemicals into our lakes, rivers, and groundwater, poisoning their inhabitants and all that drink or eat from them, including us. The entire food chain becomes contaminated. Not only are chemicals washed away, but what's left are concentrations of salt deposits, which can hurt crops and the water table. Irrigation is responsible for the drying up of the Colorado River, which now doesn't make it to the sea or to our Southern neighbors in Mexico who once relied on the river for their agriculture, too. (To find out more about the troubles with irrigation refer to chapter 4.)

We also know that the traditional practice of growing only one type of crop over a large area, known as "monoculture," leaves crops vulnerable to blight. Planting many crops together provides the strengths of biodiversity. Crops not only protect and enrich one another, their variety also provides an economic safeguard for farmers, for if one type of crop is wiped out, farmers have other choices.

FACT: ACCORDING TO STATISTICS FROM THE EPA, PESTICIDE SALES INCREASED FROM $500 MILLION IN 1962 TO $11.9 BILLION IN 1997.

"FRANKENFOODS"

Remember Dr. Frankenstein, who dabbled in science and ended up creating a monster? The monster resulted because Dr. Frankenstein couldn't fully understand the ramifications of his endeavor. The same goes for genetic engineering or modification of foods, when companies scientifically modify crops so that they are resistant to pests, contain more nutrients, are modified to depend on purchasing specific fertilizer and pesticides from the same agribusiness, or are spliced with fish genes to make foods (like tomatoes) with shinier skins that last longer.

Proponents of "biofoods," or GMOs (genetically modified organisms), feel that these altered crops could more adequately feed the poor and help farmers stay afloat.

Biofoods are a new phenomenon, and at this time we don't know all of the ramifications of altering nature like this. We don't know if the pests can develop an immunity to biofoods, like they can with pesticides. What we do know is frightening. Bio-eradication of these pests can go too far and cause a loss of food source for other animals, creating a reaction on a larger scale throughout the food chain.

FACT: THE LOSS OF HABITAT CONSTITUTES THE GREATEST THREAT TO THE EXISTENCE OF NATIVE CREATURES AND BIODIVERSITY. THE SECOND GREATEST THREAT IS THE BIOLOGICAL INVASION OF NON-NATIVE PLANTS AND ANIMALS.

A factor that concerns people about biofoods is the spreading of their pollen. If a genetically altered plant is introduced into nature, what are the risks to the environment? Pollen can travel hundreds of miles, and a field of biologically engineered crop produces its genetically altered pollen, which then spreads to natural plants.

Say a field of genetically modified corn is growing ten miles away from a field of unmodified corn. If the pollen from the modified corn reaches the other field, they will cross-pollinate, essentially creating a new breed of corn.

There was a public outcry in the year 2000 when a genetically modified corn patented as StarLink by Aventis CropScience Corporation leaked into the human food supply, and some feared that the genetically modified foods may be responsible for some allergic reactions. StarLink corn was engineered to produce a protein that acts as a pesticide to certain insects, and the corn has been approved by the Food and Drug Administration as food for livestock and cattle, not for people. Genetically modified corn has also been found in white corn, a variety that was thought to be invulnerable to effects from the genetically modified corn. Some GMO critics say that this validates their fears that GMO corn cannot be effectively quarantined from the food supply meant for people. Even after all of this, the FDA still approves GMO corn for human consumption.

If you don't think messing with GMOs can be dangerous, think again. Researchers found that pollen from corn that had been engineered to protect it against insects seemed to have also killed the larvae of the monarch butterfly, which feeds on the maize. These effects could be looked at as our "canary in the coal mine." Miners used to take the birds into coal mines because they were more sensitive to toxins. If the bird would pass out or die, the workers knew they needed to get out of the mine immediately. The loss of the monarch butterfly and sterilization of soil are just some of our modern-day warnings as to the dire consequences if we do not immediately change course.

Another problem with biofoods is that at this time the Food and Drug Administration (FDA) does not require companies to tell consumers if their product has been genetically altered, thus taking away our consumer power and the chance to decide. Europe was not so quick to embrace GMO foods and still requires labeling. They may ban American foods without labeling. The problem is that the EPA says the FDA should label foods and the FDA says the EPA is responsible if pesticides and herbicides are used.

When you buy a genetically modified food such as the New Leaf Superior Potato, a potato developed by Monsanto and marketed for human consumption, there is no label to tell you that its genes contain an insecticide even though the vegetable is legally registered as a pesticide by the EPA. Many of your favorite products, including "healthy" cereals, baby food, corn, and soy (even tofu), probably contain genetically modified foods, and you don't even know it. Although companies like Monsanto are trying to stop it, certified organic labeling requires that no GMOs be allowed in the product. Also, many products that are not yet certified organic have to trace their ingredients and notify the public if they are GMO-free.

OLD MCDONALD HAD A FARM, A BURGER, AND A SHAKE

Once upon a time old McDonald had a farm with cows, chickens, and goats, and all was well. Today, huge corporations have taken over many of the small farms and own thousands of acres of land to graze cows for beef for fast-food restaurants and mass consumption. E-I-E-I-O. Not exactly the happy end to a nursery rhyme, is it? Unfortunately, the ending doesn't improve. Much of the land used for grazing used to be rain forests rich with many varieties of plants and animals. In expanding their businesses, the corporations have purchased the land, burned down the forests, and destroyed all that lives in and depends on it for survival. If that weren't bad enough, the cows' gas contains methane, which contributes to global warming. Their manure can also contaminate water and contribute to algae blooms, which can kill marine animals.

Raising livestock is a major industry. Cattle are major polluters of the environment. Their overgrazing can lead to soil erosion. Without grasses to keep the soil in place, soil is blown away by wind and washed away by rain. Cattle can also kill fish in river systems by eating the plants that grow along the banks. This riparian vegetation stabilizes the banks of the river, preventing deposits of sediment from entering the water. It also provides shade and shelter for fish and other aquatic creatures. Without the plants along the banks to act as a buffer, too many nutrients, such as the fertilizing properties of manure, can contaminate the water.

Once the forests are stripped, cattle graze on the land, but since their limited diet lacks a variety of nutrients, they are given growth hormones to stimulate meat production and to increase their milk flow. Large amounts of antibiotics are also used to help control the many types of diseases, such as anemia, influenza, intestinal diseases, and pneumonia that occur when animals are kept in overcrowded conditions. Both hormones and antibiotics can enter our bodies when we eat beef or consume dairy products containing them, and companies are not required to put labels on products to alert us to the presence of these substances. Antibiotics given to farm animals also leave behind drug-resistant microbes in the meat and milk. These supermicrobes enter our stomachs with every burger and milkshake we consume. This overuse of antibiotics is creating more kinds of drug-resistant bacteria, which makes humans more vulnerable to previously treatable diseases.

MAKING THE NEWS

ONE COUPLE MADE THE DIFFERENCE

In late 1996, when their 2-year-old daughter started demanding ice cream, journalists Jane Akre and Steve Wilson began investigating rBGH (recombinant bovine growth hormone), the genetically modified growth hormone American dairies have been injecting into their cows to stimulate milk production. As investigative reporters for a Fox Television station in Tampa, Florida, they discovered that millions of Americans were unknowingly drinking milk from rBGH-treated cows. Additionally, Monsanto—the hormone manufacturer—had sued some small milk distributors, making it illegal for them to use labels promoting their "rBGH-free" dairy products.

The duo also documented how the hormone, which can cause harmful side-effects in cows, was approved by the FDA as a veterinary drug without adequately testing its effects on children and adults who drink rBGH milk. Studies were also uncovered linking its effects to cancer in humans. The longest study the journalists could find on the potential effects of the hormone was done on 30 rats for a period of only 90 days, and was conducted by Monsanto itself; the results showed lesions in many of the animals. Even though the hormone had been banned in Canada, Europe, and many other countries, rBGH was still given approval by the U.S. government.

Just before the broadcast of *Mysteries in Your Milk*, the TV station cancelled the widely promoted reports after Monsanto threatened Fox with "dire consequences" if the stories aired. The husband-and-wife team say that because they were unwilling to drop the story, they were pressured by Fox lawyers to rewrite the piece 83 times.

Akre and Wilson contend that after being faced with many "threats of dismissal" and rejecting an offer from Fox to buy out their contracts, they were fired in December 1997. Fox, on the other hand, contends that it exercised its option to terminate Akre and Wilson's employment contracts after one year because of their personality conflicts with staff and management, their inability to create a balanced piece, and their failure to produce an adequate number of stories for the station

In 1998, Akre won $425,000 in a suit against Fox for violating Florida's whistle-blower law, a statute that makes it illegal to retaliate against a worker who threatens to reveal employer misconduct. The jury voted that they thought the station terminated Akre's employment "because she threatened to disclose to the FCC under oath, in writing the broadcast of a false, distorted or slanted news report which she reasonably believed would violate the prohibition against intentional falsification or distortion of the news."

Strangely enough, Wilson, who represented himself and had virtually identical evidence, lost his case. Even though the couple spent their life's savings and had to sell their dream house to cover legal expenses, they felt that the lawsuit was the only way their story on rGBH (owned by Fox) would be released to the public. The situation also brought up a lot of ethical questions about journalistic integrity, and so expert witnesses including newscaster Walter Cronkite and public-interest advocate Ralph Nader were solicited by the plantiffs. Wilson says that the public airways are "a priviledge and a public resource to serve the public's interest. We work for the public. We didn't get into the business to cover up the truth. You know it's getting bad when the news is being controlled by big corporations."

Meanwhile, with their assets drained, both Akre and Wilson have had difficulty finding full-time work in television news. They recently formed a production company to expose environmental and health news that is increasingly ignored by mainstream media. Meeting with so much resistance within their professional field, Akre and Wilson felt honored to be recognized with a 2001 Goldman Environmental Prize. *(cont.)*

When asked if the decision to sue was tough, Akre says, "It was an easy one to make, but a much harder decision to live with." The couple say that "Even though doing the right thing doesn't always pay, we took a vow of poverty to continue to do it." They must now defend the award to Akre through the appeals process because Fox's legal counsel feels "The court applied the wrong standard when deciding this case."

No matter the outcome of the appeal, nobody can dispute that Akre and Wilson's case brought much-needed international attention to the ways in which large corporations can effect the political decision-making process as well as information dissemination through the media. Fortunately, this controversial subject also alerted us to the health problems associated with rBGH milk so that the public can make educated decisions when purchasing dairy products.

WASTE NOT, WANT NOT

There are no federal regulations for the handling, use, storage, and disposal of farm manure. So what happens to all that excrement? A lot of it gets stored in open, reeking cesspools and earthen "lagoons." For some reason, when the word *lagoon* is used in this context, images of tropical beaches don't exactly come to mind. Another way of storing the manure is underneath the livestock housing area itself. Imagine a wading pool about knee-deep filled with a liquid slurry of manure, and you'll get the idea what these receptacles look like. The third most common way of storing manure is in large, silo-type structures.

The stored manure can pose a threat because of the development of bacteria. Various gases are formed when the manure decomposes, including ammonia, carbon dioxide, methane, and hydrogen sulfide. Hydrogen sulfide is a poisonous gas that smells like rotten eggs. The most minute amount can cause dizziness, irritation of the respiratory tract, nausea, and headache. With concentrations exceeding 1,000 parts per million, death from respiratory paralysis can occur with little or no warning.

Manure can potentially cause disease outbreaks, such as in the United Kingdom, where in the year 2000 hundreds of thousands of cattle, pigs, and sheep had to be slaughtered in an attempt to contain the spread of foot-and-mouth disease, a deadly and highly contagious virus that can affect any cloven-hoofed animal.

As we discussed in the previous chapter on water, fertilizers from agriculture also wash into streams and rivers and make their way to the oceans. The phosphate-rich fertilizers cause algae blooms, which can kill or severely harm all marine life forms. This was what happened at the point where the Mississippi River drains into the Gulf of Mexico. It is currently known as a "dead zone," since fish and other marine life are not able to survive there.

Pastureland is not the only source of waste pollution from livestock. Pig, chicken, and dairy farms would be more accurately described as factories, where these animals live in cramped and inhumane conditions. Some of the manure created from these animals is used to fertilize crops, but the amount of waste far exceeds the need for fertilization.

FACT: WASTE FROM CATTLE, CHICKENS, AND HOGS HAS POLLUTED 35,000 MILES OF RIVERS IN 22 STATES AND CONTAMINATED GROUNDWATER IN 17 STATES, ACCORDING TO THE EPA.

COTTON IN THE CROSSFIRE

Agriculture and livestock are not the only farming industries that harm the environment. The cultivation of crops for fibers also does severe damage. Ah, cotton, the magic plant of fluffy clouds that gets spun into our soft sweaters, our warm, fuzzy socks. Chances are, you're probably wearing cotton right now as it is the number one plant fiber for textiles.

Growers must keep up with the world demand for cotton. To do this takes a lot of work because cotton is a high-maintenance plant. It uses enormous amounts of water and is susceptible to pests and disease. And to get a high-yielding crop, cotton also requires heavy fertilization and large amounts of pesticide. All of this before it's even harvested.

Once cotton is harvested and the fiber separated, it is bleached. Natural cotton is not the white that we associate with underwear, but a creamy tan. When white means cleanliness and purity, who wants to have underwear that's not white? So the need to bleach arises only from a marketing standpoint. Simply put, whites just sell better. But bleaching is a dirty business. The harsh chemicals used pollute our air and water, killing aquatic life. These chemicals have been linked to many health problems and birth defects.

A fiber that uses far less water to grow than cotton—and hardly any pesticides—is hemp. Hemp is one of humanity's oldest domesticated crops, with a multitude of uses ranging from the making of textiles and paper to its nutritive value as a food source. Hemp is essentially the same plant as marijuana with one major difference: hemp does not have the psychoactive properties of marijuana. In plain talk, hemp won't get you high.

So if hemp really does do all this great stuff, why isn't it used more? Because it's *illegal!* Federal law classifies hemp as a drug, because it's also the source for marijuana and therefore a controlled substance. It's strange how the government allows arsenic in our drinking supply, yet makes hemp illegal. Some critics of legalizing hemp for industrial uses say that the move to legalize is a smoke screen used by people who want to legalize marijuana. But it doesn't take a rocket scientist to see that hemp may pose a threat to big business. Industries like timber and cotton make billions of dollars each year, and it's a safe bet that they aim to keep it that way.

MAKING THE DIFFERENCE IN YOUR DAILY LIFE

The future belongs to those who believe in the beauty of their dreams.

—ELEANOR ROOSEVELT

Go organic!

Buy organic foods, on which pesticides, herbicides, and chemical fertilizers haven't been used. If you have the time, space, and inclination, grow your own organic garden.

Make meatless meals.

One of the greatest gifts you can give the planet is to choose to become a vegetarian or, even better, a vegan (no animal products whatsoever). At first, you might think you would rather eat dirt than give up your favorite BBQ ribs or ice cream sundae. That's because you're looking at what you'll be sacrificing instead of what you'll be giving the world. It's also a common misconception that vegetarians can eat only vegetables or really bland foods. You'd be surprised at the savory vegan recipes or meat substitutes you can find. If the damage to the Earth and the suffering of humans caused by our food choices are not enough to convince you to change your eating habits, consider the intense pain and suffering the animals go through in order to become food on your plate. If going "cold turkey" is too challenging at first, start by eliminating one type of meat, and work your way up to a new diet, as a reduction is better than no change at all. During this transition period, read the labels when buying meat or dairy products to find out how the animals were raised and if they were fed hormones. Look for free-range, hormone-free products where the animals were fed organic foods. After finding out all of the negative impacts of meat, dirt starts to look pretty darn appetizing in comparison.

FACT: IT IS ESTIMATED THAT 100 ACRES OF LAND CAN PRODUCE ENOUGH BEEF FOR 20 PEOPLE OR ENOUGH WHEAT TO FEED 240.

Compost your food scraps.

By composting, you produce less waste for landfills, while at the same time you are creating nutrient-rich soil for your garden or potted plants. If you don't have a garden or yard, give the soil to gardeners or needy plants in a park.

Say bye-bye to biofoods.

Since labels won't tell you if the ingredients are genetically modified, you'll need to look for a symbol on products that says ("no GMO" or "organic"). You'll have the best luck with this endeavor when shopping at a health foods store.

Wash your produce.

Use organic soap and water or organic citrus cleaners to wash excess pesticides from your produce before eating.

Use friendly fertilizers.

Aside from using compost, what can you do to create nutrient-rich soil? Bone meal, rock/colloidal phosphates, and greensand are great alternatives to commercial fertilizers with chemicals. Also, if you add wood ashes to your soil in late fall or early spring, you'll create great growing ground. Additionally, used coffee grounds and leftover black coffee has nitrogen and other nutrients that plants love.

Get wise about weeds.

Mulch is a great way to keep weeds under control without using harsh chemical herbicides. To create your own mulch, spread bare soil around your plants and then cover with tree trimmings, straw, pine, bark chips, grass clippings, newspaper, or other degradable material. This layer will prevent light from getting to weeds, thus impeding their growth. It also preserves moisture, develops into rich soil as it decays, and keeps the surface of the soil cooler, which is good for earthworms, micro-organisms, and plant roots. You can also spread landscape fabric over the soil to prevent weeds from germinating. If you already have pesky weeds, you will need to pull them out at the roots if you don't want them popping up again.

FACT: HOME GARDENERS USE UP TO 10 TIMES MORE TOXIC CHEMICALS PER ACRE THAN FARMERS.

Buy clothing made from hemp or organic fibers.

As harmless as it seems, cotton is the number one user of pesticides in the world, contaminating the air, water, land, and field-workers on all the major continents. Think twice before buying new items. Do you really need that new T-shirt? When buying cotton, also consider giving someone else's throwaway a new life instead of purchasing a new item.

FACT: ONE CROP OF HEMP GROWN ON ONE ACRE OF LAND PRODUCES THE SAME AMOUNT OF PULPABLE FIBER AS ONE ACRE OF 20-YEAR-OLD TREES.

MAKING THE DIFFERENCE IN YOUR COMMUNITY

Support local organic farmers and farm products.

These days you can have fresh organic produce delivered to your door. Look in the Yellow Pages or on the Internet. Urge chain grocery stores to carry or expand their organic selection of produce and food products. Support community- or worker-owned food co-ops.

ONE-STRAW REVOLUTION

MASANOBU FUKUOKA MADE THE DIFFERENCE

Masanobu Fukuoka is a Japanese farmer who made the difference by "doing nothing." A pioneer in sustainable agriculture, he practices and teaches what he calls the "no-plowing, no-fertilizing, no-weeding, no-pesticides, do-nothing method of natural farming." By working in cooperation with the ecology of nature, he has successfully revegetated desert lands in Africa, Asia, and Europe and produced crops with yields at least as high as those of pesticide-ridden crops. His method is based on sowing seeds of forest trees, bushes, fruit trees, green manure plants, vegetables, and grains all together before the rainy season starts. To protect the seeds from the birds and the small animals, they are wrapped into clay balls, called pellets. The seeds are thrown on the land and stay in their clay covers until the environmental conditions allow them to germinate. One year later, the plants that will survive will be the ones adapted to the local conditions.

Fukuoka was born in 1914. He studied Western sciences of microbiology and plant pathology and worked as an agricultural customs inspector in Japan until he became seriously ill. After his illness, he came to realize that "human knowledge was meaningless." He has written the books *One-Straw Revolution* and *The Natural Way of Farming,* which go beyond simple descriptions to embody the philosophy on which his farming is based. In 1998, at the age of eighty-six, he received the Magsaysay Prize (the "Noble Prize" of Asia) for his contribution to the well-being of humanity.

Nuture your neighborhood.

Start or join a community garden.

Petition for transition.

Support transitional programs that help farmers learn alternatives to raising cattle. Also, buy your food locally.

MAKING THE DIFFERENCE GLOBALLY

It is never too late to be what you might have been.

—GEORGE ELIOT

End irresponsible irrigation.

Farms should be required to collect a certain percent of gray water to use for irrigation.

Support hemp for victory!

There is no good reason not to legalize hemp. Many people don't know that George Washington had huge hemp plantations and during World War II, the U.S. government launched a major campaign directed at America's farmers to grow hemp for the war effort. That campaign was called Hemp for Victory! Hemp grows easily without herbicides, pesticides, or chemical fertilizers. It can be used to make many products. Hemp fibers can be used to make rope or fabrics that look like silk, denim, or rayon. Hemp oil can also be used as a fuel alternative.

As a food, hemp oil contains a high amount of omega-3 and omega-6 fatty acids. These fatty acids are important for brain development and vision. They also play a role in preventing arthritis, hypertension, and heart disease. Additionally, hemp seeds also contain a higher source of protein than soybeans and are easier to digest.

Hemp grows like a weed, maturing quickly and requiring almost no maintenance. Two crops can be harvested in a single growing season. For making paper, it truly is a viable alternative to trees. Unlike wood, hemp doesn't have to go through the harsh chemical treatments to make paper, and it doesn't take years to grow. Hemp fiber is more durable than cotton, and when made into cloth it can have a softer texture. It is naturally resistant to pests. Hemp can successfully replace our dependence on cotton as a textile.

FACT: FASHION DESIGNER ARMANI MADE TWO HEMP SUITS FOR ACTOR WOODY HARRELSON—ONE TO WEAR TO THE GOLDEN GLOBES AND ANOTHER FOR THE ACADEMY AWARDS.

Make alternative the norm.

Our government needs to provide incentives for farmers to switch to organic methods. The methods small-scale organic farmers use now can be adopted by large agribusiness. Many organic farmers have found little to no change in the amount of production during the transition and often times increased production in the long-range because they aren't stripping the land of valuable nutrients. Farmers aren't the only ones exploring these avenues.

The New York State Department of Transportation, in its program to control vegetation along highways to maintain visibility and ensure the function of guardrails, is investigating alternatives to herbicides. Methods such as mulch mats, weed fabric, and wildflower plantings will be tested in different segments along the roadway in the Rochester Herbicide Alternatives Demonstration Project.

The government also needs to have stricter regulations on pesticides, including more and longer-range testing on the effects these chemicals can have on humans and the environment.

SILENT SPRING

RACHEL CARSON MADE THE DIFFERENCE

Rachel Carson is credited for starting the environmental movement as we know it today. This is the story of the woman who dared to reveal the truth about the danger pesticides pose to our environment.

Rachel Carson was a marine biologist for the U.S. Fish and Wildlife Service before she wrote *Silent Spring,* the book that opened Pandora's box. The title of the book was a warning that if we keep poisoning the Earth, the day will come when no birds will be left to usher in the springtime with their song. *Silent Spring* exposed the irrefutable data that pesticides were the cause of massive deaths of birds and predatory animals.

At the time *Silent Spring* was published, the U.S. government didn't even have an environmental policy, let alone a sense of environmental responsibility. The Environmental Protection Agency was created largely because of the impact Carson's book had on the world.

When *Silent Spring* was published in 1962, there was an orchestrated, all-out assault by the chemical companies, scientific community, and the world at large to discredit her. Before the book's publication, excerpts appeared in the *New Yorker,* and major chemical companies tried, unsuccessfully, to suppress the book. When it did appear, Carson was painted by critics in major publications like *Time* magazine as hysterical and alarmist. And because she was a woman, media played up the stereotype of her being emotionally fevered.

Carson and *Silent Spring* were perceived as a big threat to business as usual. Let's face it, these guys were making a killing off their policy to poison. What is truly alarming is that there are more pesticides being used today than when *Silent Spring* was published. The pesticide industry has on the most part successfully blocked and or delayed many protective measures outlined in *Silent Spring*. The apathy and outright aiding and abetting of the political establishment is nauseating.

The federal government's statues regulating pesticides and fungicides are much more lax than those regulating food and drugs. Congress intentionally made these rules harder to enforce. And once an existing pesticide is considered too toxic to be used, it usually takes from five to ten years before it is finally taken off the market.

Two years after the book's publication, Rachel Carson died from breast cancer, a disease that evidence has shown is linked to exposure to environmental pollutants. Carson's willingness to cry out against the poisoning of the Earth is a reminder *(cont.)*

that yes, one person can make a difference. This is her legacy. She showed us that corporations and the government are blinded by greed and shortsightedness. But finger pointing does not elicit change. Ultimately, we are the solution.

Carson revived the sublime wisdom of interconnection. The model of a world where humans are pitted against nature does not serve us any longer. It is time to start seeing ourselves as we truly are—humans and nature inextricably and beautifully one.

Manage the waste.

Limit the number of animal farms in an area (especially near waterways), and use the waste to create natural fertilizer.

Use your right to know.

We need more protection of animal rights and stricter testing of the effects of hormones and antibiotics on milk and meat. Additionally, the public has the right to know what is in animal products; petition for more accurate labeling. This includes labels on all products that contain genetically modified food. Find out more by reading *The Food Revolution* by John Robbins.

Boycott the beef.

The government shouldn't allow beef to be purchased from rain forest areas.

INSPIRATIONAL ACTIVITIES

★ Plant a garden or window box, or get involved in an organic community garden.
★ Give up one meat or dairy product a month.
★ Volunteer at a small local animal farm or shelter.
★ Give a prayer of thanks before eating your meals.
★ Support organic and locally grown food as much as possible.

MEDITATION

I will live my life in a way that recognizes and honors that I am what I eat and that the Earth and every living creature suffers or thrives by my food choices. The vibrancy of color and life in my food reflects in the vibrancy of my life and character.

ORGANIZATIONS AND RESOURCES

THE ALTERNATIVE FARMING SYSTEMS INFORMATION CENTER

E-mail: afsic@nal.usda.gov
Web: www.nal.usda.gov/afsic; also www.nal.usda.gov/afsic/csa/csastate.htm

FARM SANCTUARY—EAST

PO Box 150
Watkins Glen, NY 14891
Phone: (607) 583-2225
Fax: (607) 583-2041

FARM SANCTUARY—WEST

PO Box 1065
Orland, CA 95963
Phone: (530) 865-4617
Fax: (530) 865-4622
Web: www.farmsanctuary.org. They host: www.factoryfarming.com

MOTHERS FOR NATURAL LAW

PO Box 1177
Fairfield, IA 52556
Phone: (641) 472-2499
Fax: (641) 472-2683
Hot line: (800) REAL-FOOD
E-mail: mothers@safe-food.org; mothers@m4nl.org
Web: www.safe-food.org

PETA (PEOPLE FOR THE ETHICAL TREATMENT OF ANIMALS)

501 Front Street
Norfolk, VA 23510
Phone: (757) 622-PETA
E-mail: info@peta-online.org

SIX

Land of the Lost?

Considered an unofficial anthem by many Americans, "This Land Is Your Land" proclaims:

This land is your land, This land is my land,
From California to the New York Island;
From the redwood forest to the Gulf Stream waters
This land was made for you and me.

In the shadow of the steeple I saw my people,
By the relief office I seen my people;
As they stood there hungry, I stood there asking
Is this land made for you and me?

Woody Guthrie's lyrics still ask valid questions about the state of our country and world. Is our land now made only for those who can pay the highest price, such as those in the timber, mining, fossil fuel, and land development industries? What about the American Indians and the economically disadvantaged? If it's their land too, why are so many forced to live in barren or toxic environments? And will that which is left of the trees and wildlife eventually end up ghettoized in zoos and a few national parks?

MORE TREES, PLEASE!

What do environmentalists look like? Well, they must be hippies munching on granola in between protests to save the forests, right? Wrong! Nature lovers come in all shapes and sizes. In fact, you'll be hard-pressed to find anyone who will say they are *against* nature. Some may fit the stereotype described above, but others are hikers, notable scientists, famous actors, photographers, artists, or ordinary parents who want clean forests to take their kids camping, and still others might even be loggers. Even though these laborers don't fit most people's definition of an environmentalist, a growing number of those in forest industries are realizing that truly sustainable methods are in their best interest, as it means that their jobs and communities' livelihood won't disappear along with the trees.

Even though many loggers have become enlightened to the consequences of the destruction of forests and their ecosystems, still too many look at conservationists as threats to their jobs. Likewise, many activists look at the loggers, not as individuals with families to support, but as coldhearted destroyers of the planet. As long as these two groups approach each other with hate in their hearts, no resolutions can come about.

WOOD PRODUCTS

Once upon a time, wood was used for fires to keep human beings warm. Then new uses for wood were discovered. The timber could be used to build simple things, like houses, carts, and boxes. The wood pulp was used to make paper and books. Until the industrial era, the process to make such products was slow, as was the system for extracting trees. Two loggers would take a long handsaw and place themselves on opposite sides of a selected tree. Then they would push and pull the saw between them while forcing the jagged blade of the saw against the tree.

Once the tree had been felled, it was hitched to a team of horses, which would slowly drag it from the forest. As you can imagine, this was quite a laborious project, and the log still hadn't even hit the lumber mill to be processed. If we had stopped the growth of industries and population at that period of time, forests most likely wouldn't be facing the dangers they are today.

Now we have the technology to wipe out entire forests with the blink of an eye. The horses have been replaced by helicopters, which lift out the fallen trees. Similarly, our rate of population growth and production place a huge burden on wood for many different types of building materials, paper products, and wood fuel (well, some things haven't changed).

A huge amount of lumber is used for building supplies. Old-growth redwood trees, some thousand of years old, are being cut down every day so that we can have our hot tubs and fancy decks. Most building contractors use new timber instead of investing in recycled or used supplies. The main reason for this is that most companies and consumers want to choose the cheapest route for the short term, when alternatives to virgin wood are available that actually look as natural as precious woods and are more durable, thus costing less in the long run.

One of the biggest culprits in the destruction of forests is the paper industry and, in turn, all of us who waste paper products at an alarming rate. From newspaper to paper towels to product packaging, paper is a wood by-product that our society mindlessly consumes. Many people ease their conscience by assuming that the industry will simply plant more trees. Unfortunately, the saplings can't possibly grow fast enough to replace all the trees we're cutting down, especially when they aren't harvested in ideal conditions, which you'll learn about later in this section. On top of the tree issues, the manufacturing of paper products also uses a lot of water and produces deadly dioxins when the paper is bleached with chlorine.

ACTING UP

WOODY HARRELSON MADE THE DIFFERENCE

When most people think about Woody Harrelson, they immediately picture the clueless character Woody portrayed on the popular American sitcom *Cheers*. But this actor is anything but dense when it comes to what is going on in the world at large and what needs to be done to promote environmental sustainability. Unlike many celebrities, Harrelson is not simply the spokesperson for a cause, he literally puts his body where his beliefs are.

In San Francisco, California, in 1996, Woody and accomplices scaled the Golden Gate Bridge to hang a sign that read, "Hurwitz, Aren't Ancient Redwoods More Precious Than Gold?" The seventy-five-foot-wide banner referred to Charles Hurwitz's now-infamous statement at his first meeting with Pacific Lumber employees after acquiring the company in a hostile takeover: "I believe in the golden rule," he said. "He who has the gold rules." Police blocked traffic on the bridge until these brave activists were done with their business and came down four and a half hours later. The crusaders were arrested, cited, and released within a few hours. Even though their commute was slowed down, most of those stuck in the traffic jam shouted words of support.

When asked to pick a particular environmental cause from all he supports, Woody says, "The ancient forests, because it's the most pressing issue, as we can't just manufacture more after they're gone." He adds quickly that you can't single out just one environmental issue, as they are all interconnected. Woody has been arrested for intentionally planting hemp seeds in Kentucky to protest the fact that this sustainable crop continues to be illegal, despite its unlimited benefits. He even wore a hemp suit made for him by Armani to the Academy Awards to increase awareness of the cause. Woody also started the SOL (Simple Organic Living) tour, traveling with friends and family by bike, accompanied by their bus *The Mothership,* which runs on hemp oil and biofuel from vegetable oil. To top it off, it's solar powered and the interior is lined with hemp fabric.

In a world where most struggling actors take on a second job to support their dreams, it almost appears that Woody uses his acting career to support his activism. He laughs when he thinks about something he saw recently that poignantly illustrates his views on the current state of the world: "It was an American flag where the stars had been replaced by corporate logos." In the same anticorporate vain, Harrelson tells a story about how he was at a friend's house recently when his friend pointed out that Woody was wearing shorts with a trendy corporate logo on them. He looked down and was a bit surprised to find it was true. Without further ado, Woody shimmied out of his shorts and left them in a heap. He'd rather go bare than wear a symbol of what he calls "the beast."

Even though to Woody Harrelson "everyone who breathes is an environmentalist," he acknowledges that many people are unable to feel, and they use drugs and other distractions "to anaesthetize themselves against an uncaring world." He feels the only way to make a difference is to "work together for a love revolution of the heart. Violent means just won't work. We need to have individual action with a cooperative vision."

In order to work toward this cooperative vision, Woody has helped to create voiceyourself.com "to connect the many voices."

DEVASTATING DEVELOPMENT

One of the largest causes of the destruction of forests and natural environments has been development. About 30 percent of the world's land has already been converted into agricultural, urban, and suburban areas. At the rate we're going, another third could be converted within in the next hundred years.

The average American uses eight times more ecosystem area than does a person in a developing nation, just to support his or her consumption. Population growth and worldwide increases in consumption are two of the largest pressures on ecosystems.

Trees are just as important for an urban ecosystem as a natural one, as they remove thousands of tons of pollutants from the city air, keep the region cool during hot summer days, and reduce the noise levels in the urban jungle. Additionally, city forests also provide invaluable areas for relaxation and recreation. Unfortunately, poor urban planning and pollution are constant threats to these respites.

COWS IN THE RAIN FOREST?

When people imagine the rain forest, they may picture monkeys, lush foliage, and towering trees. Most don't think of cows. Unfortunately, the cattle industry is leading the destruction of the rain forests. Farmers wanting to supply cheap beef to the Western world cut down and sell the trees, burn whatever is left, and use the barren land for cattle grazing. The responsibility for this lies largely with the governments who fail to promote sustainable agricultural practices as an alternative to forest clearance. Often the government actually subsidizes the conversion.

FACT: SINCE 1950, OVER HALF OF THE WORLD'S TROPICAL FORESTS HAVE BEEN LOST.

FACT: IN PENINSULAR MALAYSIA, MORE TREE SPECIES ARE FOUND IN 125 ACRES OF TROPICAL FOREST THAN IN ALL OF NORTH AMERICA.

FACT: AN AREA OF RAIN FOREST EQUAL TO THE SIZE OF A FOOTBALL FIELD IS DESTROYED EVERY SECOND OF EVERY DAY.

Another business that should be concerned with the destruction of the rain forests is the pharmaceutical industry, which makes an estimated $300 billion a year off plants and roots taken from the rich ecosystem. For example, a plant called the rosy periwinkle, which grows in the rain forests of Madagascar, has been used to make a drug that can cure some kinds of cancer. Imagine what other potential cures could be wiped off the face of the planet along with the forests.

FACT: IN A PHARMACY, 1 IN EVERY 4 PURCHASES WILL CONTAIN AN INGREDIENT EXTRACTED FROM A TROPICAL FOREST.

RAVAGING THE RESOURCES

As you can imagine, where destruction of the environment is taking place, the petrochemical industry can't be far away. Much virgin wilderness is devastated when companies come in and drill for oil or natural gas. A lot of the deforestation in the tropical rain forest and forests around the world is caused by those who build roads and camps and drive their destructive machinery through the ecosystem. What they extract is a nonrenewable resource: something that took thousands of years to create can be destroyed in a matter of days. The mining industry is as destructive as the fossil fuel companies, and they also use toxic chemicals in their practices, which get into the water supply and are absorbed by the trees. Additionally, in places such as Africa, war, death, and starvation are all fueled by lust for gold and diamonds.

Now that you have a better understanding of what leads to the destruction of forest lands, discover the rippling effects of such actions.

CULTURE CLASH

Many tribes and cultures make the rain forest their home. They depend on its ecosystem for their livelihood. When the forests are destroyed, these people not only lose their means for supporting themselves, they can also lose their traditions and ways of life. Whether they collect nuts and berries or use herbs for healing, all that they know can be taken away with the forests.

FACT: THE AMOUNT OF WOOD AND PAPER WE THROW AWAY EACH YEAR IS ENOUGH TO HEAT 50 MILLION HOMES FOR TWENTY YEARS.

SLASH-AND-BURN

Another huge issue with deforestation is the methods used in the industry. When timber companies clear-cut, they do not just take selected trees in an area, they cut down or destroy all of them. This means that the wildlife and plants that depend on the trees for shelter or nutrients are also killed off or displaced. Even a decomposing log is essential to the habitat, as many insects live in it and it provides nutrients to the soil for new trees and plants to grow.

Frequently, after an area is clear-cut, it's burned completely. This technique is called slash-and-burn. It's done in both agricultural farming and when planting new trees to make "nutrient-rich" soil. Even though the land may be enriched in the short term, this technique generally doesn't work in the long run because the top layer of dirt is highly susceptible to erosion and, without plants and roots to keep it in place, can be easily washed away. Also, the chemicals usually used in these techniques strip the soil of all its nutrients, including destroying important microorganisms in the soil. Many people don't understand the value of old-growth trees and the intricate ecosystems they support. Those who are ignorant are under the impression that if we cut down trees, we can always "just make more." Unfortunately, it isn't that easy to recreate what Mother Nature has already perfected. We wouldn't consider killing off our grandparents and replacing them with youngsters!

FACT: ABOUT 30 PERCENT OF THE CARBON THAT ACCUMULATES IN THE AIR EACH YEAR COMES DIRECTLY FROM THE CONTINUED BURNING OF THE RAIN FORESTS.

After planting new seedlings, the timber companies often neglect the newly planted areas, and the budding trees are strangled to death by weeds. Even worse, most companies dowse the entire area with toxic herbicides, using diesel fuel as an adherent. Additionally, reseeded areas are generally populated with only one species of plant. These monocultures are extremely vulnerable, as they lack the support, nutrients, and protection that the original polyculture provided. In a forest with only one type of tree, you will lose the diversity of all other plants and animals as well. This also means that all of the trees are susceptible to the exact same hardships, including insects, so they can easily be wiped out.

Another problem with the killing of the forests is that we're also threatening a great symbiotic relationship we have with plants. Plants produce oxygen, which we breathe in, and they absorb carbon dioxide. Fewer trees means less oxygen. Additionally, slash-and-burn produces a lot of carbon dioxide, which contributes to global warming.

Another issue with clear-cutting and timber practices is that when everything has been slashed and burned there isn't any life left to absorb all the excess rainwater. This can cause terrible problems with erosion, landslides, and the destruction of watersheds. The soil washes away into a river, damming it up and smothering the aquatic life. Mud slides can displace families, destroy homes, and even kill people and animals. Likewise, the destruction of watersheds (in addition to the herbicides and pesticides) can cause water contamination and contribute to flooding.

CRITTERS OF THE WORLD, UNITE!

As you can imagine, the destruction of the forests and any natural environment can cause the extinction of many wildlife species. One of the hottest debates over this took place in Headwaters Forest in northern California, as it contains the last stand of unprotected old-growth redwoods and is considered crucial habitat for threatened species such as the coho salmon, steelhead, marbled murrelet, and the spotted owl.

For hundreds of thousands of years, the wild coho salmon have returned from the ocean to the Pacific Coast, bringing with them large quantities of nutrients for humans, animals, and plant life. A combination of impacts, including overgrazing, river mining, urban and industrial pollution, agricultural diversions, and urbanization have contributed to the coho salmon becoming extinct in more than half of their native rivers.

Because they spend so much time in freshwater, the coho salmon require excellent upstream habitat. Siltation (excess dirt and debris) and temperature increases are the primary factors in their decline. Logging along the Pacific Coast has caused far-reaching damage to coho habitat. Reduction of shade cover heats up the stream temperature to lethal levels for the fish. Siltation caused by logging roads and erosion from logging activities in streamside areas made the stream channel too warm and muddy for the salmon and their eggs to survive. The proliferation of mud slides along the coast of California and Oregon have meant loss of life and property every year. The slides all too often originate on steep, recently clear-cut slopes.

After years of pressure from the environmental and fishing communities, the National Marine Fisheries Service finally listed the coho in California as threatened under the Endangered Species Act, with much opposition from the timber industry, agribusiness, and state governments.

BIRD OF PARADISE

ROSALIE EDGE MADE THE DIFFERENCE

Rosalie Edge was a veteran of the movement for women's suffrage, with well-honed political action skills, when she took on the corrupt Audubon Association in 1929. Her passion for birds had led her into the conservation movement. While in Paris, she heard of the collusion between Audubon directors and commercial wildlife harvesters and returned to New York to use her considerable political skill and dedication to uncover and stop the corruption. She said, "For what to me were dinner and the boulevards of Paris when my mind was filled with the tragedy of beautiful birds, disappearing through the neglect and indifference of those who had at their disposal wealth beyond avarice with which these creatures might be saved?"

She attended Audubon meetings and, during open sessions, opened fire with embarrassing, specific questions about Audubon officials' conduct. She founded the Emergency Conservation Committee (the ECC), designed to reform the Audubon Association, and successfully sued the association for access to its mailing list. She paid to publish a pamphlet detailing the misdeeds of the Audubon directors. Her focused and forceful efforts met with success. By 1934, the corrupt directors were gone and the alliance with game harvesters finished.

She continued her conservation activities throughout her life, creating a wildlife sanctuary on Hawk Mountain in Pennsylvania. When the Audubon Association resisted her pressure for them to buy the land, she raised the $3,500 herself to purchase the land for the sanctuary. She was the president of the Hawk Mountain Sanctuary until her death in 1962. Her legacy lives on in the sanctuary and throughout the conservation world.

But it's the marbled murrelet that won one of the most important environmental lawsuits ever to be based on the Endangered Species Act. The Environmental Protection Information Center had sued the Pacific Lumber Company over its plans to log its timberland in the Owl Creek area five miles southeast of the Headwaters Forest. In an unequivocal decision that should have clearly reached to the Headwaters Forest, a U.S. district court judge issued a permanent injunction to prevent the company from taking any more habitat from the marbled murrelet anywhere in southern Humboldt County. Unfortunately, even this didn't stop Pacific Lumber, since it knew that its profits made while breaking the law would outweigh the penalties. These are only a couple of examples of the many species being threatened everyday by the destrutction of their habitats.

FACT: ACCORDING TO VARIOUS SCIENTIFIC ESTIMATES, 35 TO 200 SPECIES OF LIFE BECOME EXTINCT EVERY DAY.

FACT: A STUDY HAS SHOWN THAT THERE ARE POSSIBLY OVER 30 MILLION SPECIES OF INSECTS LIVING IN THE CANOPIES OF TROPICAL FORESTS. NOW THAT'S A LOT OF BUGS!

MAKING THE DIFFERENCE IN YOUR DAILY LIFE

> The worst sin towards our fellow creatures is not to hate them, but to be indifferent to them. That's the essence of inhumanity.
>
> —GEORGE BERNARD SHAW

Be aware of building supplies.

When doing home improvements, find out where the lumber in your local building supply store comes from. Make sure it doesn't sell any wood from old-growth forests. If it does, start a petition, boycott, and organize a protest. Your best option is to find places that sell salvaged supplies or carry recycled wood alternatives.

WOOD WANNABE

ROGER WITTENBERG MADE THE DIFFERENCE

For people who think it's not economically feasible for companies to take the environmentally conscious route, think again! In 2000, Trex was ranked number one in *Forbes Magazine's 200 Best Small Companies*. This company made its success by manufacturing lumber for beautiful patios, decks, benches, lawn furniture, board walks, playground structures, marina docks, railing, fencing, landscaping, signage, and swimming-pool surrounds, yet not a single tree is cut down and no plastic is created in the production process. This is because this unique lumber is made completely from recycled plastic grocery sacks and industrial shrink-wrap mixed with what is considered "waste" wood.

The idea for Trex originated in the late 1980s, when chemist Roger Wittenberg worked in Philadelphia making animal feed from bakery waste. He became irritated that he had to pay for the leftover plastic wrappers to be taken to the dump. Wittenberg says, "I was in the bread crumb business, and I made lots of bread crumbs. And when you make lots of bread crumbs, you have lots of plastic bread *(cont.)*

wrappers left over. [Trex] is the solution for what to do with all those bread wrappers."

This entrepreneur then heard of a company that was struggling to make fireplace logs from waste wood. The ingredients of the project suggested a recipe for wood-polymer lumber, so Wittenberg cooked up a company he called Rivenite to make it.

Then, in 1992, Mobil Chemical Company bought Wittenberg's business and hired him as technical manager for the Composite Products Division. Four years later, the division was thriving, and Wittenberg and three of his co-workers bought it from Mobil. Wittenberg became head of research and development for the newly born Trex Company.

Now, annually, about half the plastic sacks recycled in the United States are trucked to the Trex plant, south of Winchester, Virginia. This is more than 150 million pounds of plastic that would otherwise end up in landfills each year. Along with waste industrial shrink-wrap, the bags are pulverized, mixed with an estimated equal amount of sawdust, and then melted to make a wood-polymer lumber. Trex gets its plastic from recycling programs and the sawdust from wood waste supplied by furniture, pallet flooring, and cabinet manufacturers.

Even though Trex reflects the environmental mottoes of reusing and recycling, it doesn't use this fact to market its products. The company knows that customers (primarily contractors) are more concerned about quality and price than about saving trees and recycling waste.

Fortunately, Trex wood-polymer lumber meets all these requirements. It's as dense as natural wood, but the boards don't splinter or rot and are impervious to weather and insects. Since the lumber has high wood content, it has a nice appearance and is not slippery. Additionally, it has UV protection and contains no preservatives, chemical additives, or virgin wood.

Project costs are comparable to jobs done with high-grade cedar or redwood, and when upkeep is figured in, Trex is actually less expensive than natural wood. This revolutionary lumberlike material is so well respected that it has been used on the boardwalk in Atlantic City, for walkways at Mount Rushmore National Park and the Florida Everglades, and also at Disneyland. One of the best qualities of Trex is that the company also has its own recycling program; any product that is no longer needed can be recycled yet again.

Preserve the paper.

Reuse and recycle your paper products. When purchasing paper, look for 100 percent postconsumer recycled content or paper made from hemp or kenaf fibers. Instead of subscribing to the newspaper or magazines, read them on-line or at your public library. Carry your own cup so you don't need to get coffee or your beverage of choice in a paper cup. Use a reusable cloth grocery bag instead of disposable paper ones. Don't buy items with excess cardboard or paper packaging.

FACT: IF WE ALL RECYCLED OUR SUNDAY NEWSPAPERS, WE COULD SAVE MORE THAN HALF A MILLION TREES EVERY WEEK.

Explore the alternatives.

Instead of wasting paper made from trees, use kinds of paper made from hemp or kenaf fibers.

Get off junk mailing lists.

You know you don't want most of the flyers and leaflets that clutter your mailbox anyway, so reduce the amount you receive (by up to 75 percent) by writing to:

Mail Preference Service
Attn: Preference Service Manager
Direct Marketing Association
PO Box 3079
Grand Central Station, NY 10163
Or do it on-line at: www.the-dma.org/cgi/offmailinglistdave

FACT: AN ESTIMATED 4 MILLION TONS OF PAPER JUNK MAIL ARE SENT EACH YEAR IN THE UNITED STATES, AND NEARLY HALF OF IT IS NEVER OPENED.

Go green.

If you're not already, consider becoming a vegetarian. You don't have to go "cold turkey"; feel free to wean yourself off meat gradually. You'd be surprised at how many tasty meatless meals you can make. Begin by avoiding beef, especially from fast-food restaurants, where it may have come from former rain forest lands.

Shop smart.

Don't buy products that come from endangered animals or plants, even if the marketing proclaims it will give you extra-potent sexual prowess or eternal youth. These are the types of promises that lead to the extinction of species.

MAKING THE DIFFERENCE IN YOUR COMMUNITY

> **Mankind has become a locustlike blight on the planet that will leave a bare cupboard for its own children—all the while in a kind of Addict's Dream of affluence, comfort, eternal progress.**
>
> —GARY SNYDER, *TURTLE ISLAND*

Organize your office.

Insist that your office manager purchase only postconsumer recycled paper. When buying it in bulk, you can often get a discount. If you don't have recycling bins at your workplace, call a recycling center to find out how you can set them up. Instead of tossing out paper that's been used on only one side, save it to use the other side.

Use it in your printer or copy machine when making printouts for yourself or others in an informal context.

Buy locally.

Buy products made locally so you know how they are made. It not only supports your community, it also reduces the chances that rain forests were destroyed in the manufacturing process.

Keep an eye on development.

Read your local newspaper and participate in community meetings so you know what building development plans are in the works. This way you can alert residents if valuable nature areas are at risk. It also gives you the opportunity to talk with construction companies about the virtues of lumber alternatives.

Extinguish the flames.

Avoid making fires as much as possible, and when making one, try salvaging for scrap wood (from the forest floor) and used paper instead of using commercial firewood.

MAKING THE DIFFERENCE GLOBALLY

You can't shake hands with a clenched fist.

—GANDHI

Find common ground.

Finding common ground doesn't mean environmentalists must compromise what they're fighting for. To make progress, both loggers and conservationists must keep building bridges—with a foundation of love, compassion, and respect—that can span the gap between the two sides. Although this is a huge challenge, simply opening the lines of communication is the first step toward creating a win-win situation.

Hopefully, from these conversations the laborers and unions will recognize the importance of sustainable forestry for their own livelihood as well as that of our planet.

Trust your land.

Many landowners are unaware that they can get significant tax breaks by donating their land to a trust so the area and environment will be protected in perpetuity or can be used for research on real sustainable forestry. Spread the word about land trusts.

Work toward sustainable solutions.

Slash-and-burn techniques need to be eradicated and replaced with sustainable forestry methods. To get it started, governments need to offer significant incentives to industries that transition to a more respectful and less impactful form of logging. Additionally, the leaders in rain forest regions need to educate landowners about the economic benefits of harvesting truly sustainable and renewable resources (like nuts or rubber) and subsidize the process. The latest statistics show that rain forest land converted to cattle operations yields the landowner only $60 per acre, and if timber is harvested, the land is worth only $400 per acre. However, if these renewable and sustainable resources are harvested, the land can yield the landowner $2,400 per acre.

States should also offer career transition programs for loggers and mill workers to move into new trades, especially types of work that are not only environmentally sound but also support their communities and families (even during the winter months).

Value all creatures, great and small.

Laws need to be put in place to protect animals that are endangered by development. No logging should be allowed in habitats with threatened wildlife.

Punish the poachers.

Serious penalties need be put in place for poachers. In the Serengeti of Tanzania those caught killing wildlife may receive up to thirty years in prison. Unfortunately, if they have enough money and meet a corrupt official, they might be able to buy their freedom.

Share your gripes with the government.

Demand from our government that all old-growth forests be protected from deforestation. Officials also should enforce stricter policies and punishment for logging companies when they break environmental laws. With the current system, it's often cheaper for the logging industry to pay infraction fees than adhere to the regulations. We also need to let them know it's not okay to drill in pristine natural regions to get to oil and natural gas. Additionally, our country needs to boycott beef that comes from rain forest cattle.

Request "opt-in only" marketing mailers.

Petition the U.S. Postal Service so that it becomes illegal for marketers to add your name and address to their mailing lists unless you've "opted in" to receive particular information. It should be illegal for companies to sell or trade personal information they've collected about you.

MEDITATION

I will live my life in a way that honors trees and forests as deeply sacred by greatly reducing my consumption of every piece and every form of paper and wood.

Standing with your feet firmly planted on the ground, stretch your arms high into the air. Take a deep breath in, and release the deep breath out with the sound of wind. Wave your arms in the wind of your breath like branches of a tree as you give thanks for the all the gifts that trees offer, including clean air to breathe, a stable climate, and water gathering, storing, and release.

ORGANIZATIONS AND RESOURCES

CIRCLE OF LIFE FOUNDATION

PO Box 3764
Oakland, CA 94609
Phone: (510) 601-9790
Fax: (510) 601-9788
E-mail: info@circleoflifefoundation.org
Web: www.circleoflifefoundation.org

EARTH ISLAND INSTITUTE

300 Broadway, Suite 28
San Francisco, CA 94133
Phone: (415) 788-3666
Fax: (415) 788-7324
Web: www.earthisland.org

ECOLOGICAL PANEL

100% Recycled Wood
PO Box 273 Piazza Imperatore Tito, 8 20137
Milano, Italy
E-mail: info@panneloecologico.com
Web: www.pannelloecologico.com

INSTITUTE FOR SUSTAINABLE FORESTRY

SmartWood contact info:
46 Humboldt Street
Willits, CA 95490
Phone: (707) 459-5499
Fax: (707) 456-1851
E-mail: isf@igc.apc.org
Web: www.isf-sw.org

NATIONAL AUDUBON SOCIETY

700 Broadway
New York, NY 10003
Phone: (212) 979-3000
Fax: (212) 979-3188
Web: www.audubon.org

NEW LEAF PAPER

(supplier of recycled paper for this book)
Phone: (888) 989-LEAF
E-mail: info@newleafpaper.com
Web: http://www.newleafpaper.com/

RAINFOREST ACTION NETWORK

221 Pine Street, Suite 500
San Francisco, CA 94104
Phone: (415) 398-4404
Fax: (415) 398-2732
E-mail: rainforest@ran.org
Web: www.ran.org

SIERRA CLUB

85 Second Street, Second Floor
San Francisco, CA 94105-3441
Phone: (415) 977-5500
Fax: (415) 977-5799
E-mail: information@sierraclub.org
Web: www.sierraclub.org

WORLD WILDLIFE FUND

World Wildlife Fund
1250 24th Street, NW
Washington, DC 20037
Phone: (202) 293-4800
Web: www.worldwildlife.org

SEVEN

Environmental (In)Equality

Success is not measured by the position one has reached in life, rather by the obstacles overcome while trying to succeed.

—BOOKER T. WASHINGTON

Historically, low-income communities have been treated unfairly when it comes to environmental regulations. Because these communities can't hire fancy lobbyists to argue their cause, a disproportionate share of landfills, incinerators, and other pollution-causing projects are placed in their neighborhoods. We need to achieve equal justice for all people regardless of race, gender, or sexual orientation and in all areas of life, including the environment.

Now we must look into our communities. What can we do to make them strong, vibrant, happy, healthy, and safe? Take the time and the initiative to find out what issues are facing your community, for example, urban sprawl and overdevelopment, water and air pollution, big business agriculture, destruction of natural places including city parks and trees, industrialization and privatization of prisons and schools—the list goes on and on.

Once you educate yourself on the issues, pick one or more that most resonate with you, and get involved. Form alliances, especially with the least likely candidates. They are the ones we all need the most. We must extend our consciousness and actions beyond our lines of privilege. Environmental and social issues are first and foremost attacks against the poor and historically oppressed and marginalized peoples. Although environmental degradation does not discriminate, it is only the privileged who can afford to fend it off with safe, clean drinking water and organic foods or to fix it with good hospital care. Community must extend to include everyone, of every background and culture in the world.

STANDING TALL

JOANN TALL MADE THE DIFFERENCE

JoAnn Tall, a member of the Oglala Lakota tribe on the Pine Ridge Reservation in South Dakota, has dedicated herself to improving the lives of the Lakota people and preserving their sacred land. As a mother of eight and sufferer of severe rheumatoid arthritis, she has overcome challenges and made many sacrifices to take on threats to the well-being of her people and indeed all people and the planet. She was inspired by prophetic dreams and spiritual experiences to begin her fight by raising awareness about the dangers of local uranium mining and a proposed Honeywell nuclear weapons testing site.

When JoAnn spread word of the dangers of the proposed Honeywell site through her radio station and put up a resistance camp of tepees and a sweat lodge at the proposed site, Honeywell abandoned its plans.

She went on to cofound the Native Resource Coalition, which serves the Lakota people with research and education on issues related to land, health, and the environment. When the AMCOR Company proposed building a 5,000-acre landfill and incinerator on the reservation, JoAnn inspired tribal members to pressure the tribal council to reject the proposal. She also spread her influence and information to other reservations across the country to encourage them to fight against dumps on their land. She currently serves on the board of directors of the Seventh Generation Fund and continues to inspire people around the world to fight for their health, land, and planet.

MAKING THE DIFFERENCE IN YOUR DAILY, LOCAL, AND GLOBAL LIFE

The horizon leans forward, offering you space to place new steps of change.

—MAYA ANGELOU

The best thing you can do to fight environmental injustice is to stay educated on where potentially harmful industries are located in your community or around the world. Check out www.scorecard.org to find a comparison of neighborhoods based on environmental burdens felt by different racial/ethnic and income groups. Just type in your ZIP code to find out how your area rates. If you find incidence of environmental inequality, contact officials or start a petition or boycott. If you still aren't heard, get media attention, send out press releases, or learn how an act of civil disobedience could be used to make a change for the better.

CHILDREN FOR A SAFE ENVIRONMENT

KORY JOHNSON MADE THE DIFFERENCE

In 1989, when Kory Johnson was nine and a half years old, her sister died at the age of sixteen from heart problems that were likely caused by contaminated well water her mother drank while pregnant. When Johnson attended bereavement support groups, she discovered that many families in her neighborhood had lost loved ones and that the area was a cancer cluster. Kory decided that she could not stand by and let this happen to her community. She formed Children for a Safe Environment (CSE), which now has 359 members and fights ceaselessly for environmental justice. *(cont.)*

CSE's first battle was to take on the enormous ENSCO hazardous waste incinerator and dump that was being planned for a poor Arizona community. The group teamed with Greenpeace Action, wrote letters, educated the public, protested, demonstrated, and planned children's art projects to fight the incinerator. In1991, the governor of Arizona canceled the incinerator plans.

Johnson now travels around the country, speaking on behalf of children like herself from minority communities that are being harmed and endangered by pollution and waste. She has continued to take part in many effective campaigns, including a fight against the dumping of DDT-contaminated dirt from a California Superfund site in Mobile, Arizona.

Kory sums up her dedicated struggle: "Young people everywhere are entitled to environmental justice, no matter what their color or socioeconomic status. My sister died when I was nine and a half, and that is when I started Children for a Safe Environment. Ten years later, with a lot of victories behind us, we still fight the same fight every day: environmental justice."

INSPIRATIONAL ACTIVITIES

- ★ Get a map of your town or city. Then call your city officials or look on-line to find out where dump sites, sewage treatment, and power-producing plants are located. Mark them on the map, and see if you find a correlation between these points and poverty-stricken or racially segregated locations. If there is a link, let others know, and do something about it.
- ★ Look at the advertising billboards in poor or racially segregated areas. How do the products pushed differ from those in the more upscale or Caucasian districts?

MEDITATION

Beginning with hands at heart center, palms together, slowly wave hands as if they are a ripple first forward, then moving out to your sides, arcing upward, and then back to heart center. As you do this meditation, think about all of your daily actions and how they ripple out into the world, affecting people's lives and the planet.

Let us honor diversity in all its forms—plant, animal, and human. I recognize that environmental degradation is an attack first against the poor and historically marginalized and oppressed peoples, traditionally people of color. I will live my life in a way that recognizes that my choices ripple out into the world, affecting others' quality of life.

ORGANIZATIONS AND RESOURCES

ONEWORLD USA

Benton Foundation
950 18th Street, NW
Washington, DC 20006
Phone: (202) 638-5770
Fax: (202) 638-5771
E-mail: us@oneworld.net
Web: www.oneworld.org

GREENACTION

1540 Market Street, Suite 325
San Francisco, CA 94102
Phone: (415) 252-0822
Fax: (415) 252-0823
E-mail: greenaction@greenaction.org

ENVIRONMENTAL JUSTICE RESOURCE CENTER AT CLARK ATLANTA UNIVERSITY

223 James P. Brawley Drive
Atlanta, GA 30314
Phone: (404) 880-6911
Fax: (404) 880-6909
E-mail: ejrc@cau.edu

EIGHT

Speaking Up Makes the Difference

To believe in something, and not to live it, is dishonest.

—MOHANDAS K. GANDHI

HOW TO GET MEDIA ATTENTION

Publicity means telling your story—and capturing the attention of the eyes, ears, and even hearts of people, lots of people. The tough thing is, it's noisy out there, and you need your story to get through. But like most things, beginning with small steps is the way to approach a media campaign. If *campaign* is too scary a word, think of it as a plan—a plan that targets how best to tell your story, and get your story out there, for maximum impact for your cause.

Step 1: Plan with a Purpose

The first step in any media campaign is to think about why you need media attention and, most important, what you hope to achieve with the resulting publicity.

Is your goal to

★ Raise awareness about your cause? This is great, but be even more specific. What do you want people to know? In a world of short attention spans and information overload, what is the primary message you need people to understand?

★ Provide a counterargument? Perhaps your aim is to refute a commonly held belief. If so, your goal is to provide credible, accessible alternative information to counter the prevailing misconception.

★ Instigate action? Ideally, your publicity will invite and excite people to take action. Again, this is terrific, but specifically what action(s) would you like to see your new acolytes take? Sign a petition? Write a company or legislator? Boycott a product? Start recycling? Change their buying or TV-viewing habits? What?

Step 2: Craft Your Message

In addition to clarifying your objectives, decide what specifically you want to publicize. Do you want to

★ Attract publicity for your cause?
★ Generate publicity for your program(s) or an upcoming event?
★ Make a startling announcement?
★ Simply tell your story in a powerful, maybe even provocative, way?

Don't try to accomplish all of these objectives with just one message. The more specific and detailed you can be, the more interesting it will be to both media folks and the public.

Your Cause Célèbre May Be Célèbre Only to You.

It's important to find a "hook" for your story. Keep in mind that media folks are unlikely to provide coverage for your cause unless there's some compelling new, fresh, or local angle on the story. Look for something or someone that makes your issue or organization especially relevant or timely.

In preparing for your media blitz, consider developing a one-page fact sheet and a press release (see later).

Fact Sheets

Create a one-page document that carries the salient facts about your program. When was it founded? Who benefits? How many people do you serve? What geographical area do you cover? How many staff do you have? Who is the director? And don't forget your address, phone number, and Web site, if you have one.

Do not try to pitch your program here. Keep it short and sweet. A bullet-list format is the best.

Radio PSAs

Radio PSAs (public service announcements) are those short announcements you hear on the radio between commercials, usually late at night. But don't be discouraged; radio stations have listeners at 2 A.M. A PSA calls for very tight writing. It should be written so it can be read aloud, at a normal pace, in ten seconds. Practice with a watch. (You can also send a thirty-second spot, but it will have lower chances of being read on the air.)

Television PSAs

If you can interest a local television station in shooting a thirty-second spot about your programs, this is the most effective way to tell your story. It's not easy to do this, however. Television production is expensive, and stations will be hard to convince. But, hey, you never know unless you ask! If you decide to produce a spot on your own, enlist a professional to shoot and edit it; don't try to do it on your camcorder!

Step 3: Develop a Media List

Stop! Before you try putting together your own list of all the news editors, reporters, and news directors covering your area of interest, check to see if such a list already exists. You may be able to find an existing list in your community, and if you do, be sure to check that it is up to date.

If you can't find a list, do it yourself. You can begin in the library by looking at a copy of the *Editor and Publisher Yearbook,* with listings of the top editors in daily and weekly newspapers. Also see their on-line directory of links to publications.

You can also get information by looking at the mastheads of the newspapers in your area and by telephoning television and radio stations to ask who should receive your mailings. This is hard work, but it will pay off by producing a terrific list.

Step 4: Work the Web!

Don't forget the power and potential of the Internet for getting the word out. You might try

- ★ Planning a targeted e-mail campaign
- ★ Posting messages in appropriate newsgroups where your message would be relevant and welcome
- ★ Publishing and promoting your own Web site, soliciting cross-linking relationships with related sites (affiliate marketing)
- ★ Instigating an e-mail- and letter-writing campaign to decision makers, companies, and legislators
- ★ Building a LISTSERV (electronic mailing list)
- ★ Creating an e-newsletter
- ★ Initiating and monitoring an e-petition
- ★ Starting a boycott campaign

Step 5: Follow Up

The hardest thing to do is one of the most important—calling the editor to ask if he or she received the release or PSA and asking if there are any questions. Be prepared to send the editor another release. Remember that these folks get releases by the barrelful.

Once you've made your first contact, go on to experiment with other elements in a typical media campaign:

- ★ Draft a letter aimed at decision makers for use in an on-line or off-line letter-writing campaign.
- ★ Draft a letter for editors of local media, or write an op-ed article.
- ★ Contact the producers or hosts of local talk shows.
- ★ Try getting a local or national celebrity interested—or invested—in your cause.
- ★ Investigate building a Web site, or if a Web site already exists, look into promoting the site on- and off-line.
- ★ Distribute an e-newsletter.

HOW TO CREATE A PRESS RELEASE

As the currency and cornerstone of public relations, press releases are an excellent (and relatively cheap) way to get your message out to the media, and ideally, to the public. They are essential to any media campaign. With a well-written press release, and a little patience, you can put your cause on the media map and in the public eye.

What is a press release? It is typically a one- or two-page document that argues why your organization or cause should be featured in the media. It won't help to go out and buy expensive, coral-speckled letterhead to make your case. The most effective format for a press release still is plain black type on basic 8 1/2 x 11 white paper.

"DON'T BE A WEENIE"

TERRI SWEARINGEN MADE THE DIFFERENCE

In 1990, a registered nurse named Terri Swearingen cofounded the Tri-State Environmental Council, a coalition of grassroots citizen groups. She was inspired by concern over the carcinogenic heavy metals emitted by the largest toxic waste incinerator in the United States. This was an incinerator built by Waste Technologies Industries in a low-income residential neighborhood on the banks of the Ohio River within 1,100 feet of an elementary school and 320 feet from the nearest home. Terri began traveling across the country, speaking to communities endangered by toxic facilities. She wound up her tour with a demonstration in front of the White House, where she was arrested for civil disobedience. The very next day the White House announced major changes in regulations for overseeing the nation's toxic waste incinerators, following the steps proposed by Swearingen earlier that year. A nationwide moratorium on new incinerators was initiated and old regulations overhauled.

In her ongoing campaign against incinerators, Terri has become an expert in creatively using the media to focus the attention of the community on the issue. She understands that the media is more likely to cover events, especially those with a flair of the spectacular, than to report on the nitty-gritty of citizen research. When a newspaper called then-governor of Ohio George Voinovich a "weenie on waste," she seized on his new nickname and mounted a "weenie" campaign, with a series of hot dog–wielding demonstrations, a weenie roast on the governor's lawn, stickers about the issues placed on hot dog packages in supermarkets, and wieners sent regularly to the governor. Demonstrators would attend the governor's speaking engagements wielding foot-long hot dogs, on one occasion embarrassing him so much that he canceled the speech. Terri recommends this type of punchy and spontaneous approach to others trying to draw attention to important issues because she has seen and proven that it works.

A good press release is

- ★ *Newsy.* Straight news stories, packed with facts or quotes, are widely used by most media outlets.
- ★ *Helpful.* Magazines, newspapers, and television and radio stations appreciate press releases containing tips, techniques, or strategies for the reader or listener. You can often call attention to your cause under the guise of simply offering useful tips.
- ★ *Topical or trendy.* Always try to capitalize on a current event or widely discussed trend.

Step 1: Craft Your Press Release

The first words at the top of your press release should be *For Immediate Release* and the date or *For Release on.* A request to delay, or embargo, a news release is usually respected by the press, unless the news you are describing is not controlled by your organization.

Also at the top, you will need to write *For more information, contact* and the name of the person who will answer questions from the media. Give his or her telephone numbers and e-mail contacts, if available. It is always best to have a couple of people so that if one person is not available, another is.

Although styles vary, a press release needs the name of your organization and its address and contact information. The words *News Release* or *Press Release*, or something similar, should be near the top.

Step 2: Write the Press Release

Remember high school journalism? Include Who, What, Where, When, How, and especially Why. Give it a strong lead—one that will grab attention. A good press release follows what is known as an inverted-pyramid format. That means: Begin with the most important information. Then move on to a quotation to back up the first paragraph, or add something slightly less important, such as a fact related to your major news. Is your group planning a direct action? Put this near the top, and let the editors know if it is part of a broader movement and is tied to external news or is purely local.

If your release goes over one page, type *MORE* at the bottom of the first page. Then retype the title and the date on page 2, so it is clear with which release page 2 goes. At the bottom of page 2, type -30- or -#-, to signal the end. The release should be no longer than one and a half pages; news agencies prefer one page, though. A little can go a long way. Always double-space, and make it sharp and easy to read. Here are some basic press release types:

- ★ An announcement of an upcoming event
- ★ A list of contacts that can serve as useful news sources to reporters covering a news story close to your organization's mission
- ★ The release of a publication or launch of a new Web site for your cause
- ★ Commentary or reaction to a news event related to your mission
- ★ A speech, or new research, delivered by someone in your organization (Send this type out in advance with an embargo, to delay the release until the speech or research has been made public by you.)

Step 3: Grab Attention

If you want a press release that will not only capture the media's attention but woo your target audience, try these tips:

- ★ *Create a colorful headline.* Most editors will read a press release based solely on the headline. A good headline gets to the point and says why your news is important. Avoid promotional sounding words.
- ★ *Don't bury your lead!* Always lead your press release with the essential *who, what, where, when, how,* and *why.* Use this paragraph as an abstract or summary for the release, but keep your abstract interesting!

- *Use quotes instead of hype.* This is a good place to make your case most poignantly. If you draft a quotation for someone in or associated with your organization, make sure this person approves it first.
- *End your press releases with contact information.* Give your readers a call-to-action. Include a name, address, phone number, URL, and e-mail in the last paragraph of the release, even if this repeats information you gave at the top.
- *Find a hook.* Don't expect every publication to pick up every release you send. Editors and news directors receive piles of paper every day. Your material needs to stand out in some way. Are you solving a problem or filling your readers' needs? Pinpoint that need or problem, and write from that perspective. If you can, humanize the press release by telling the story of a particular person or place.
- *Always put yourself in the reader's shoes.* Help editors understand why your news is important to their readers. Be sure you "go local" if you're working with a local publication. That means putting in names of local people involved with your cause. If you're sending your release to business publications, make sure you address issues that concern business-section readers.
- *Send your release to an actual person.* Don't address your mail to "Editor" if you can find out easily that her name is Sarah Jones. Try to cultivate some relationships in the media. No matter where you live, don't discount the weeklies and suburban papers. Often the chances of getting a story there will be greater than with a daily paper.
- *Again, keep it short!* One page is better. Two pages are an absolute maximum and you shouldn't have more than 500 words. One great and free way to learn skills for writing effectively is by researching "letters to the editors" of newspapers and magazines. They usually have a 200-word limit, so it teaches one how to create a clear and important message with limited space. Letters to editors are free advertisement for an issue. Plus, everyone loves to read them because it's a way of knowing what others in your community are thinking and feeling. The more people who express concerns or thoughts about a particular issue, the better chance you have of getting a letter on that topic published.

START A PETITION DRIVE

Petitions have quite an impressive history. Thomas Jefferson's Declaration of Independence, for instance, collected just fifty-six signatures, and that started a ball rolling, to say the least. Petitions are great ways to spark attention and action. The Internet is a superfast and easy way to collect names, though there is a lot to be said for old-style direct contact.

Is a Petition Right for My Issue?

Petitions can be used for a lot of actions, such as to change laws and company policies, organize unions, or to start a candidacy.

There are many types of petitions. To run for office independent of a political party, you should research your state's election rules at the election commission.

To introduce a bill to your legislature or get a measure onto a ballot, you need to find out if your community or state uses the initiative and referendum processes.

To ignite public interest or pressure others into action, you will probably need a standard petition with a statement and signatures.

Step 1: Target the Powerful

Where's the power in your particular issue? Who can take the actions you want? Find out, and put the names of the individuals and organizations you're targeting at the top of the petition statement, then send them the petition. This will show all sides where the petition is directed and what's wanted of whom.

Step 2: Write the Petition Statement

Make the language direct, professional, and attention grabbing. Explain the situation clearly, and make it compelling. It could be useful to talk to those who are on your side to discover the most convincing approach. Keep the statement short and straightforward, but keep extra information on hand to answer more detailed questions. Don't forget that even if people don't sign, creating awareness of your issue can be invaluable.

Include in your petition

- ★ Your group's name
- ★ Numbers on each signature line for counting

Step 3: Collect, Collect, Collect!

Find places where the most like-minded people are likely to pass by. If your petition is about public transportation, go to a bus stop. If your petition is about global warming, find Internet chat rooms about global warming or other environmental issues, get names, and recruit volunteers to boost your power.

Of course, it's great to get a lot of names. But don't worry about ferreting out every last signature if time is important. Make sure to complete the petition process before any important meetings or election days that may affect your issue. There's no perfect number of signers except the one that achieves your goal.

Be sure to

- ★ Have signers print as well as sign their name and include their address or telephone number.
- ★ Find out the rules set by the organization to which you're sending the petition. For instance, government offices generally won't count the names of nonresidents or, in some cases, those not registered to vote. To try to get a candidate on a ballot, ask the appropriate state elections commission for its rules.

Step 4: Turn Them In

Make copies of your petitions, including a set for yourself, and then deliver copies (or originals) to the recipients listed on your petition. To increase your impact, send them to the news media, relevant organizations, advocacy groups, and elected officials.

Step 5: Follow Up

Don't back off. Meet with those you sent the petition to, and ask them what they plan to do about the issue. Call a public meeting that focuses on your issue. Meet with local newspaper editors and radio and television producers to get some media interest.

Here are some sites where you can look at other petitions or put yours on-line:

www.petitiononline.com

www.moveon.org

CONTACTING AN OFFICIAL (A.K.A. WORKING WITHIN THE SYSTEM)

Many people either are intimidated by the idea of contacting a public official or are under the misconception that giving officials a piece of your mind won't make a difference. Remember that governmental officials are supposed to be working for us, and if the public doesn't tell them what we want, we have no chance of getting it.

Before contacting the official, get clear in your mind what you really want him or her to do for you. Do you want to know how this person stands on an issue? Do you want this leader's support or opposition on a specific issue? The more distilled your desires are, the easier it will be for you to find the individuals who might be able to help you.

It can be challenging to figure out if the issue you want to address should be directed to local-, state-, national-, or international-level officials. You might want to start by contacting your local officials and those who represent the district where you live, as they are likely to respond more quickly and may be able to guide you to someone at a higher-up level.

You might also want to brush up on your basic government processes and procedures and learn more about how the executive, legislative, and judicial branches of the federal government work. You can also surf the Internet to visit the

White House, U.S. Senate, or U.S. House of Representative sites. Additionally, you may find great information on Web sites put out by your town, city, or state.

Most regions hold regular meetings during which the public can get informed on issues and have more access to the officials. Watch for these opportunities, and use your civic entitlement to speak up. You can also use these meetings to deliver a written message or arrange a media event or protest.

Keep yourself informed about the issues you care about. Get on mailing lists and e-mail lists of organizations that share your views. Track the progress of bills.

The main telephone number for all members of Congress is (202) 224-3121. Ask for the member by name. You will probably end up leaving a message with a staff person there who will pass it along. Make sure your message is clear so as to not dilute your issue.

If you are trying to meet legislators in person, the best time to reach them is generally during a congressional recess. After an important vote or action is a good time to thank your representative or to express your dissatisfaction with the vote and to let the official know that you'll continue to work for change.

After a bill is introduced, hearings are held to obtain public and special-interest views. When the bill is first assigned to a committee, you might want to contact your representatives if you would like them to cosponsor the bill. The more cosponsors a bill has, the more likely it is to gain support and be voted into law.

It's good to contact your legislators after a bill clears the committee and before it comes up on the House or Senate floor. This is the time to let them know how you want them to vote and why.

If a bill passes in both houses, it goes into "conference," where a joint committee works out any differences between the Senate and House versions. The final version then goes to the president to be signed into law. If the president vetoes the bill instead, a two-thirds vote in both houses is required for the bill to become law. Your letter, e-mail, or call to the president may be read by a staff person who records and tallies the information as part of a comprehensive report. You may not get a personal response, but your point of view will be noted.

You may have more impact on elected officials by banding together with people who are concerned about the same issue you are. Rather than meeting with an elected official alone, you might want to try to organize a group visit or arrive with a petition.

If you are working the executive branch—your mayor, a state agency, or a regulatory arm of the federal government—think of it as a public corporation. It may be small or large, but its main goal should be customer service.

Each of the government's regulatory agencies has specific rules that any citizen or interested party must use to get heard. Check with the agency's public-information office either by phone or on-line to find times or places for public comment or procedures for submitting written comments or requests.

Work with any nonregulatory agency in a professional way, as you would with any business entity. You can request information over the telephone or, if asked, in writing. Always send major requests, such as for specific research on your topic, in writing. Log your requests and any responses you get. Move to the higher levels of authority if you are not getting the service you need further down in the bureaucratic hierarchy. Above all, persist, and save any anger for when it is truly deserved. If you put up the offensive, the receiving party will most likely be put on the defensive.

The judicial branch provides its unique service to constituents by trying criminal and civil cases. You can research the federal judicial branch's operations, but don't come to court expecting to lobby judges. Based on the courts' constitutional independence, there is no process for influencing judges' actions, unless the judge or justice is being nominated and is subject to hearings or unless you live in a state that conducts judicial elections.

If the direct approach to public officials doesn't work for you, or if you are looking for complementary tactics, try spreading the word in other ways that will indirectly affect officials' decisions. Share information about pending legislation with friends, family, co-workers, or others who care about the same issues; post fliers on bulletin boards; call in to talk radio shows; and write letters to the editor of your local newspaper.

NONVIOLENT PROTESTING

When you've exhausted all other options, sometimes the only choice is to take a direct action that may or may not be legal. Throughout history, passive resistance has been used by many groups and individuals to fight injustices, from Africans to American Indians to the Vietnam War protesters, from Rosa Parks and Martin Luther King Jr. to Gandhi, who was a strong believer in the idea that action needs to be accompanied by love. Some activists choose more radical means of getting their points across that may include more violent means. However, remember that anger often begets more anger and violence among both the protesters and the organization they are trying to change.

Protests might mean carrying, for weeks on end, picket signs that demonstrate your views, or it could mean putting your body on the line by chaining yourself to a building or tree. When choosing to participate in acts of civil disobedience, you must weigh your commitment to your cause against the potential results, as you may be arrested or face physical injury or financial hardship. You must look deep within your heart and see if you can live with the potential consequences if you choose to act or turn away from an issue that's close to your spirit. If everyone gave up because of fear or obstacles, change would never occur. The greatest acts of courage and social change throughout history have come when people were willing to put their hearts and actions where their beliefs were.

Tips for nonviolent protesting:

- ★ If planning a direct action, get nonviolence training first (from RUCKUS or another group) to learn how to get your message across without getting hurt.
- ★ Educate yourself on your rights.
- ★ Avoid physical violence and verbal abuse.
- ★ Don't wear jewelry or carry sharp objects.
- ★ If grabbed by security or the police, drop anything you're holding, sit down, and link arms and legs with the people around you. Be aware that this might result in bodily harm.

- ★ If being carried off by the police, go limp like a rag doll. Likewise, this may slow down police efforts, but may result in injury.
- ★ If you're being hurt, be vocal about it so the officer and others around you know what's happening.
- ★ If things begin to escalate, emphasize to fellow protesters and the police that it's a peaceful protest even though you mean business.
- ★ If you witness an arrest or assault, note it, and write down what happened as soon as possible. Ask for the names of officers, as they are required by law to give these names to you.
- ★ If you get arrested, remember that you do have the right to remain silent, and you have the right to an attorney.
- ★ Above all, keep calm, and face anger and violence with love and respect in both your actions and words.

For more information on civil disobedience, contact:

THE RUCKUS SOCIETY

4131 Shafter Avenue, Suite 9
Oakland, CA 94609
Phone: (510) 595-3442
Fax: (510) 595-3462
Web: www.ruckus.org

ORGANIZATIONS AND RESOURCES

One vote makes the difference! Find out how and where you can vote in your community:

FEDERAL ELECTION COMMISSION (FEC)

999 E Street, NW
Washington, DC 20463
Phone: (800) 424-9530
For the hearing impaired, TTY (202) 219-3336
Web: www.fec.gov/

ROCK THE VOTE

10635 Santa Monica Boulevard
Box 22
Los Angeles CA 90025
Phone: (310) 234-0665
Fax: (310) 234-0666
E-mail: mail@rockthevote.org
Web: www.rockthevote.org/

As you've read throughout this book, fighting for campaign finance reform is one of the best things we can all do to help the environment. Find out more:

THE ELECTRONIC POLICY NETWORK AT *THE AMERICAN PROSPECT*

5 Broad Street
Boston, MA 02109
Phone: (617) 570-8030
Fax: (617) 570-8028
E-mail: epn@epn.org
Web: www.epn.org/

THE CENTER FOR RESPONSIVE POLITICS

1101 14th Street, NW
Suite 1030
Washington, DC 20005-5635
Phone: (202) 857-0044
Fax: (202) 857-7809
E-mail: info@crp.org
Web: www.opensecrets.org/

COMMON CAUSE

1250 Connecticut Avenue, NW, #600
Washington D.C. 20036
Phone: (202) 833-1200
E-mail: grassroots@commoncause.org
Web: www.commoncause.org/

CAMPAIGN FINANCE INFORMATION CENTER

138 Neff Annex
Missouri School of Journalism
Columbia, MO 65211
Phone: (573) 882-2042
Fax: (573) 882-5431
E-mail: cfic-comments@ire.org
Web: www.campaignfinance.org/

CAMPAIGN FOR AMERICA

50 F Street, NW, Suite 1198
Washington, D.C. 20001
Phone: (202) 628-0610
Fax: (202) 628-0598
Web: www.campaignforamerica.org/

DESTINATION DEMOCRACY

Web: www.destinationdemocracy.org/

GRANNY D.

(At age 90, she walked across the United States to support campaign reform)
E-mail: burke@fastq.com
Web: www.grannyd.com/

PUBLIC CAMPAIGN

1320 19th Street, NW, Suite M-1
Washington, D.C. 20036
Phone: (202) 293-0222
Fax: (202) 293-0202
E-mail: info@publicampaign.org
Web: www.publicampaign.org

EPILOGUE

The Circle of Life Makes the Difference

I think back to my first night preparing to sit in the ancient redwood Luna. I was so jumpy, I felt like my nerves were about to burst out of my skin. I was excited, scared, nervous, and curious all at the same time. When my hiking mates and I stood at the bottom of the mountain, looking way up to its top where the tree-sit awaited, an overwhelming feeling came over me: "I can't do this. This is way too much for me. What was I thinking?" Then I looked around, seeing that I was surrounded by only guys, and I remembered growing up with two brothers and no sisters. If there was one lesson that taught me, it was, "The one thing you do not do as the only girl in a group of guys is wimp out!" Funny, where our inspiration comes from sometimes. I took a deep breath and said to myself, "One foot at a time, Julia. That is the way to climb a mountain."

I share this story because I know that as human beings we all reach points of feeling completely overwhelmed. Too much information. Too much to do. How can I, as one person, make a difference in all this? People often come to me and say, "Julia, I can't believe what you did. I could never do that." I always feel my face breaking into a grin because you could not have paid me enough money that first night to make me believe that I would be able to go through such an intense experience. If I had seen what was coming, I would have gone screaming in the opposite direction. But you see, luckily for us, life does not show us everything at once. I did not live 738 days in a tree all at once, crammed into one moment; it was one day at a time, one moment at a time. For me, it became an incredible "one breath, one prayer at a time." I know from my experiences that when our hearts open, we can find the courage to do things that our minds will always say are too difficult. After all, the root word for *courage* is *cour,* which means "heart." The more our spirit opens, the more strength and conviction we will discover we hold inside. It all begins, though, with the first step—doing the right thing because it is the right thing to do, regardless of the outcome. Striving to be a part of the solution instead of the problem.

I believe we all have our own "personal tree to sit in." For me this means committing to waking up every morning and asking ourselves, "What can I do today to make the world a better place?" And then doing the best we can to live our beliefs. As we are human, some days our best will be better than others. We will make mistakes, and then we can give thanks for the lessons they teach us. One breath at a time, one step at a time, we will find we have crossed our own perceived boundaries and limitations into a whole new divine way of living and being.

Life is a circle in which all energy flows. Every positive choice, no matter how big or small, touches all other life with healing and beauty. When people ask me how I remain so optimistic in a world in which so much is going wrong, I reply, "Eternal optimism joined with loving action is the most powerful tool I own." It is not always easy. But I grow stronger and clearer in vision every time I hold that tool in my heart and life. For this incredible lesson, I give thanks.

Begin today. Today is the day in which every moment counts. We can offer our lives in loving, joyous service to the world. Our lasting legacy is the life we leave behind. *One does make the difference. You are the one.* And you are not alone. Together, as one, we are changing the world. Congratulations and thank you, thank you, thank you.

In service of Life in Love,

Julia Butterfly Hill

INDEX